MW01121919

# CHOOSING
# RIGHT

# CHOOSING RIGHT

by
Deborah Van Dyken

Cape Lookout Publications, Inc.
Beaufort, North Carolina

Published by Cape Lookout Publications, Inc.

Book Cover by Susan Mason

Library of Congress Catalog Card Number:
Copyright Pending

ISBN 13:

978-0-9800438-1-5

Printed in the United States

First Edition, 2008

Do unto others as you would have them do unto you.

—Jesus Christ

The beginning of wisdom is calling things by their right names.

—Confucius

Misfortune, nobly borne, is good fortune.

—Marcus Aurelius
as quoted by Robert E. Lee

# Acknowledgements

I am very grateful to Biff Mahoney, publisher, and Denise Foster, editor, of our local weekly newspaper, The Gam, for the opportunity to write my family law advice column on which this book is based. Biff and Denise have been great to work with, and I have truly appreciated their support.

I also want to thank my husband, Bill Blair, for patiently listening to me read these columns to him as soon as they were hot off my printer and for his perceptive comments about them.

Finally, I want to thank my mother, Nell Van Dyken, who was also my 5th and 6th grade school teacher, for helping to instill in me a love of reading and writing and in whose class I wrote my first book.

# Foreword

I am a divorce attorney in Beaufort, North Carolina, and so, I am a story teller. For many years, I have stood up in court and told the judges about my clients' experiences of love, betrayal, pain, fear, and loss. I have also written their stories in my legal pleadings which were filed with the court. Additionally, I have listened to thousands of other cases in my sixteen years of practice while waiting for my own cases to be heard.

So, with all of that information in hand as well as my own somewhat overly vivid imagination, I began writing a family law advice column for our town's weekly newspaper, The Gam. The columns in this book appeared in The Gam in 2007.

I wrote the letters as well as my responses, but in each column, there was a family law legal point that I was trying to teach to my readers. I also juggled facts and made up lots more in each column so that my clients' right to attorney-client privilege was upheld.

Each column is based on North Carolina family law and case law which controlled at the time that the column was written. Since statutes and case law change all the time, my readers need to know that my advice in these columns may no longer be correct.

Since no book by an attorney should be without a CYA disclaimer, here is mine:

Dear Readers,

Do not rely on my advice in these columns since the North Carolina statutes and case law may have changed since I wrote these columns.

If you have a family law legal problem, be sure to see a family law attorney, and do not use the information in this book as a basis for self-help behavior.

Also, each state has its own family law statutes and case law, so readers who are not in North Carolina need to realize that their states' family law statutes and case law could be completely different from those of North Carolina.

There is one last thing that I wanted to mention since I have learned it well as a family law attorney.

Every act of kindness and every act of meanness usually has a far greater impact on far more people than was first imagined.

In a divorce, a husband and a wife have the ability to do great harm to each other since they know each other's strengths and weaknesses well. If one or both spouses also decide to use their children as their weapon of choice against each other, they have the ability to utterly destroy these children.

And people do it all the time. The real cost of such behavior can be seen in juvenile court, drug rehab facilities, mental hospitals, and the morgue.

But people have a choice in how they behave towards each other.

If spouses treat each other fairly and honestly, and try to end their marriage in a decent manner, they will save themselves much grief and heartache, not to mention legal fees. Their children will also do much better emotionally as numerous studies of divorced children have found.

So, the bottom line is that what goes around, comes around.

People need to keep that in mind as they decide which path they want to follow.

Deborah Van Dyken
July 13, 2008
Beaufort, North Carolina

To my husband, Bill Blair,

The love of my life.

# TABLE OF CONTENTS

Page

# CONTENTS

CONTENTS 19

# AS YOU SOW, SO SHALL YOU REAP

**January 4**

I think that the troubles all began last year when my wife went without me to her tenth college reunion. There, she apparently blew on the embers of an old college romance. Then, she came back home and told me all about it including the fact that her old flame was a woman.

That was bad enough, but what was even worse was that my wife told me that she wanted to have her girlfriend move into our house and become "our girlfriend", if you know what I mean.

At first, I said no, but then, the more I thought about it, the more I thought that it might not be such a bad idea after all. That was big, bad mistake Number One.

So, my wife's girlfriend moved in and became our girl friend. At first, I thought that I was having the sweet ride on the gravy train because our girlfriend was a lot younger and easier on the eye than my wife, but that was before I made big, bad mistake Number Two.

Big, bad mistake Number Two struck when our girlfriend got pregnant with twins. Naturally, my wife said that it was all my fault which from a strictly biological standpoint is one-half true, but my wife made me do it with our girlfriend, so I think that my wife started the whole thing and that this pregnancy is mostly her fault.

Now, my wife and our girlfriend are going to childbirth classes and decorating the nursery together while I am the odd man out. Neither of them are speaking much to me, and at their request, I am now sleeping on the sofa. They have even started to call me "SD" which is short for "sperm donor".

To add insult to injury, my wife recently told me that she wanted me to move out and pay her alimony because she is going to quit her well-paying job and stay home with the babies when our girlfriend goes back to work after the babies are born. How weird and unfair is that!

Do I have to move out of our house and pay my wife alimony?


ANSWER: As for moving out of your house, you do not have to leave and your wife cannot make you get out of the house unless she files a law suit for a divorce from bed and board and can convince a judge that she is the wounded, virtuous, and financially dependent spouse and that you are the financially supporting spouse who has committed wretched acts of marital misconduct.

I think that your wife might have a few problems spinning a tale of her virtuous behavior based on what the sleeping arrangements have been in your house lately.

As for alimony, your wife will also have to file suit in court for alimony. Very likely, she will have an uphill climb to get alimony since she is currently working in a well-paying job and is continuing to commit adultery with The Communal Girlfriend.

However, you have also committed adultery with The Communal Girlfriend, so the judge might find that the pot is calling the kettle black here, look at your respective financial positions, and award your wife alimony. Consequently, you are not out of the woods as far as alimony is concerned.

In fact, you are in the middle of the woods and heading for the quick sand!

In order to avoid making any further big, bad mistakes, you need to stay in your house, and you need to run, not walk, to the nearest family law attorney and get some good legal advice on how to extricate yourself from the mess that you are in.

Just keep in mind that you, and no one else, are responsible for your own actions, and that you are now reaping what you have sown.

# SHOPPING AROUND

**January 11**

My wife and I have been married for 22 years, and over time, we have drifted apart. She does not share any of my interests which are football, basket ball, and baseball, and she has made no effort to learn anything about my favorite teams and their players. I have tried to explain to her the various rules of the games and talk to her about why she should be interested in them, but she just gets this irritated look on her face, says "yes dear", and then, leaves the room when I finish speaking.

During the last two months, I noticed that my wife was gone a lot on Saturday and Sunday afternoons when my games were on. When I asked her where she was, she said that she was out "shopping".

Somehow, I just knew that something was wrong, so I began to follow her whenever she would leave to go "shopping". It made me mad to have to leave the house because I missed a lot of good games, but I knew that I had to try and find out what she was up to.

However, my wife never knew that I was right be-hind her every time that she left our house because "stealth" should be my middle name. I followed her everywhere and saw that she was usually going shopping alone, but three times, she met this same man for drinks at a bar in Atlantic Beach.

They would have one or two drinks and talk and laugh a lot together, and then, she would get in her car and come home. I had to put the pedal to the metal to get home before her, but my wife never knew that I was watching her the whole time.

I just know that my wife is cheating on me and is committing adultery with this man. I have marked down all the times that she has met this man at the bar on my calendar. I am thinking of secretly putting a voice-activated tape recorder in her car and another in our house so that I can hear all of her telephone conversations that I know that she is having with this man.

If I can figure out a company to do the testing, I want to have my wife's panties tested for semen so that I can prove her adultery. Do you think that this is a good idea?

ANSWER: I think that you need to stop all of this "stealthy" behavior and ask yourself if you still want to be married to this woman.

If you do, you need to turn off the TV, stop stalking your wife, and ask her to go with you to a marriage counselor to see if you can save your marriage.

If you choose this path, be prepared to change some of your ways and plan to spend at least as much time doing things with your wife that she enjoys as you do watching your ball games. You might also want to talk to a family law attorney so that you understand the legal implications of what you are doing in staying with your wife.

If you do not want to be married to your wife or are not sure, you still need to stop this "stealthy" behavior. Instead, you need to see a family law attorney who can advise you on the best way to document your wife's meetings with this man and what steps you need to take to end the marriage.

A private investigator would be a far better choice to document your wife's behavior with this man than to have you hovering around your wife in stealth-mode. Additionally, do not put a voice-activated tape recorder in her car or in your house so that you can record her phone conversations with this man because without a court order, you will be in violation of wiretapping laws.

Finally, don't stoop to having panty raids of your wife's dirty lingerie. If you do engage in this sort of behavior, it will be clear that you will not win any mental health awards this year.

Before going any further, the big question is how important is your marriage to you. Talk to a therapist and/or an attorney about this issue and don't do anything weird in the meantime.

Remember, separate in haste and repent at leisure.

# DO IT RIGHT OR NOT AT ALL

**January 18**

My girlfriend and I have been going out for a while, and so now, she wants to get married. So, I said, "OK. Let's get married. You pick the date." And she said "Whoa – not so fast! Where's the ring?" So, I said, "Ring? What ring? You don't think that I have to get you a ring, do you?"

Then, she looked at me with this steely look and said, "When people get engaged, the man has to give the bride-to-be an engagement ring." I said, "Next thing you know, you'll be wanting me to get down on my knees and propose to you." And then she said, "What's wrong with that?"

I knew that the conversation was going downhill fast, so, I left and went looking for an engagement ring.

I soon found out that they want a whole lot of money for just a little diamond engagement ring, and I don't want to spend that much money on a ring.

So what I need to know is whether I can just get her a cubic zirconium stone on the engagement ring and tell her that it is a diamond ring because I know that she will never know the difference.

If I do go ahead and blow a lot of money on a real diamond engagement ring, I want to make sure that if the engagement or the marriage doesn't work out, I get this diamond ring back because I don't want to spend all this money on a diamond ring for nothing if we break up before the marriage or get divorced.

What do you think?  Can I just sort of fake the diamond part of the ring and get a genuine cubic zirconium because I figure that what my girlfriend doesn't know won't hurt her, and can I get the ring back if I buy her a real diamond ring and the engagement or the marriage doesn't work out?

ANSWER: Lies and fraudulent behavior are bad ways to start an engagement and a marriage.  If you really want to be engaged and married to your girlfriend, you need to buy her a real diamond engagement ring and not some imitation stone that you try to pawn off to her as the real thing.  Do it right or don't do it at all.

As for getting the engagement ring back if the engagement is ended and no marriage occurs, there is no clear cut answer because there is no statute or case in law in North Carolina on this point.  However, tradition and case law in other states hold that if the engagement is broken at the request of the man through no fault of the woman, then the woman gets to keep the ring as a sort of consolation prize.  If the woman ends the engagement or if her behavior results in the end of the engagement, she is supposed to return the engagement ring to the man.

As for getting the engagement ring back if the marriage falls apart, you can forget it because an engagement ring is property that the wife receives before the marriage, and so, the engagement ring is her separate property. Consequently, the wife gets to keep her engagement ring, and this ring is not included in the division of marital property during the divorce.

However, it seems to me that you are asking the wrong questions about your engagement. Before you get down on your knees or not, before you get a genuine cubic zirconium engagement ring or not, before you lie to your girlfriend about the ring or not, you and your girlfriend need to get some pre-marital counseling so that you can be sure that marriage is a good decision for both of you.

Be certain that you want to get married for the right reasons so that you don't later think of this engagement ring and your wedding ring as links in a ruinous ball and chain around your life.

# THE PERILS OF DECEIVING THE DECEIVER

**January 25**

When he told me that he loved me and would marry me some day, I believed him. But time passed, and we moved in together, and still, he would tell me that he loved me but was not yet ready to get married. After two years of listening to this silver-tongued devil, I stopped asking him about marriage but I still thought about it all the time.

I began to hope that if I got pregnant, he would marry me. So, I stopped taking my birth control pills without telling him and was pregnant within a few months.

When I told him about the baby coming, I thought that he would be happy, but he was furious. He smashed a bunch of my dishes in the kitchen, packed his stuff up, moved out of our house in Smyrna and back in with his mama in South Carolina, and left me high and dry.

Well, our baby, a son, was born, and my ex-boyfriend never even came to the hospital to see the baby even though he is the father and is on the child's birth certificate. During the last year, he has hardly had anything to do with our son until this month when I decided to call and ask him for child support.

When he heard that I was going after him for child support, my ex-boy friend told me that he was not going to pay child support, that he wanted his rights as a father, that he was going to take the child away from me for him and his mother to raise in South Carolina, that I would end up paying him child support, and that there wasn't a thing that I could do to stop him from taking the child to South Carolina.

There is no custody order for my son, so I am really afraid that my ex-boy friend will come and get my son when my son is at day care. What can I do to keep my son with me in North Carolina?

ANSWER: Unfortunately, you are finding out the hard way that an out-of-wedlock pregnancy is not a guaranteed one-way ticket for a walk down the aisle.

Tricking Mr. Deceiver into becoming a father was incredibly unfair to him and also, more importantly, to your son.

None-the-less, Mr. Deceiver should not be allowed to snatch the child and carry him off to South Carolina for his mama to raise so that Mr. Deceiver can avoid paying you child support.

You need to immediately file for custody of your son in North Carolina. You also need to ask for an emergency custody order giving you temporary custody because Mr. Deceiver has threatened to take the child from his home state of North Carolina to South Carolina.

Don't delay on this one because if Mr. Deceiver got hold of the child and left to go to South Carolina with him, it will cost you a lot of time, money, and anguish to get him back – not to mention the trauma to your son.

Get a custody order giving you custody of your son so that if Mr. Deceiver then decides to take the child across state lines in violation of the North Carolina court order, he can have the interesting experience of being criminally charged with parental kidnapping in federal court. His mama will have to bring her pocketbook and a lot of plastic to help him deal with that one.

So, get this custody order in North Carolina, and in the meantime, don't let Mr. Deceiver or his mother see the child until you have the temporary custody order in hand. Your child needs to be protected from further foolish, selfish, and immature behavior by both of his parents.

# DON'T JUST TALK THE TALK – BE SURE TO WALK THE WALK

### February 1

Last year, my wife began telling me that she needed more personal space to pursue her spiritual path. So, she went on numerous spiritual retreats and weekend workshops and even changed her name to something unpronounceable which she says means "Pearl of Light" in Hindu or something like that.

Six months ago, my wife told me that it was her destiny to work full-time on her spiritual path. Unfortunately, that path led her to pack up her yoga mats and walk out the door, leaving me and our three year old daughter behind.

During the last six months, my wife has lived with five other people in a run-down house, and she has worked full-time as a "life coach" counseling people on how to find spiritual fulfillment in their lives. She also continues to go away on lots of "spiritual retreats".

Over the last few months, I have asked her to give me some child support because I am paying for our daughter's day care and health insurance, and these things don't come cheap. However, my wife just says that she doesn't have any money because these workshops are so expensive, and so, she can't afford to pay me any child support now, but will help me out later on if she has any money.

I need child support now but cannot afford an attorney to take my wife to court. What should I do?


ANSWER: First of all, the path that your wife is on is one of selfishness and irresponsibility, and I am not sure where it will lead her but it won't be any place good.

Secondly, your daughter deserves and has a right to be the financial support of her mother. Your wife has her priorities wrong if she chooses to pay for "spiritual workshops" rather than the care of her child.

As for hiring a lawyer to get child support, you don't need to because you can get your county child support office to file suit on your behalf against your wife to get child support. Their services are free or close to it, so you should contact them right away and get the child support ball rolling straight at your wife.

You need to use your county child support office to give your wife a little "workshop" so that your wife learns that part of her path in life involves the regular and meaningful financial support of her daughter.

# THE SWINGING PATH TO CHILD SUPPORT COURT

**February 8**

After seven years of marriage and two children, my husband and I were kind of getting bored with each other, and the romance had gone out of our marriage. So, my husband suggested that we try doing a little swinging since he had the seven year itch and wanted to do a little scratching.

Reluctantly, I agreed, and my husband went on-line and went full speed ahead. He even got me to do a web site where I called myself "Mystic Dawn" and had all kinds of photographs that were pretty hot, if I do say so myself. We were just getting into the swinging groove when my husband fell hard for one of the women we had "entertained".

I couldn't believe it when he left me and the kids for that little tramp. He moved from my bed right to the bed of that sorry home wrecker. I went ballistic, but it didn't do any good. My husband says that he is gone and is staying where he is because he is so in love with her. I can't understand it because she looks like she just got beat with an ugly stick and was rode hard and put to bed wet for years.

The only good thing is that my husband has agreed to give me sole custody of the kids and to pay child support to me. He is also willing to use the North Carolina Child Support Guidelines in figuring out the amount of child support that he should pay.

However, my husband is demanding that he get the two children to claim as exemptions on his state and federal taxes which his is filing separately from me this year. He says that he will be paying a ton of child support to me so he should get the two deductions for our kids. Otherwise, he says that he will be forking over lots of money in child support and not getting anything in return.

I would like to claim both children this year because I work full-time as a secretary, don't' make much money, and can get more money in tax refunds if I file as head of household with two kids. What should I do?


ANSWER: Since the scratching has stopped and Mr. Scratch & Swing has left, he is obligated to pay child support to you for the care of the children.

The North Carolina Child Support Guidelines are based on the assumption that the person who has primary physical custody of the children and who receives child support gets the state and federal tax exemptions for all of the children. So, you should get the tax exemptions for your children because you have primary physical custody of the children and Mr. Scratch & Swing should be paying you child support.

My guess is that Mr. Scratch & Swing will not want to "give" you both child support based on the North Carolina Child Support Guidelines and the tax deductions. Rather than having endless conversations with him on this issue, you should just go to your county's Child Support Enforcement Office and get them to start child support proceedings against your husband. Then, they can get a child support order using North Carolina Child Support Guidelines, and you will also get the tax deductions for the children.

However, you need to be proactive in this tax thing, so you should file your taxes as soon as possible and claim both of the children as tax exemptions. Additionally, you might consider a less self-destructive form of scratching if you come across the seven year itch in a future relationship.

# DRUNKS AND KIDS DON'T MIX

### February 22

Two years ago, I left my husband when I could not stand his drinking another minute. He would start drinking bourbon every weekday as soon as he got home from work and would not stop until he was drunk as a skunk and passed out on the sofa.

The weekends were a nightmare. My husband would get together with his drinking buddies and "watch the game" which was another way of saying swill liquor together until they were blasted and looked like they had been hit in the tail with a rotten apple.

So, I left. My husband and I decided that we would share custody of our then 11 year old son, and we alternated custody every other week. I had my lawyer draft this custody agreement into a court order which we all signed, but this custody arrangement is not working out.

Despite his big promises, my husband still drinks like a fish when he has custody of our son. My son, who is now 13, has told me that he finds liquor bottles hidden all over my husband's house and that my husband sips liquor from a plastic cup when my son is with him because my husband thinks that my son doesn't know what is going on with my husband's drinking.

During the last year, my son has told me that my husband has on several occasions been drinking and then drove my son to various school functions. I spoke to my husband about this problem, but my husband has denied that he has driven our son in the car after he has been drinking. My husband says that our son is just making this all up because my husband had just punished our son for some bad behavior. Obviously, someone is lying, and I bet that it is my husband because my son is a pretty truthful kid.

The situation is getting out of hand because last week when my son was with my husband, I got a call from the police department to come and get my son because the police had just arrested my husband for driving under the influence and my son had been in the car with my husband at the time of his arrest. I immediately went to the police station and got my son who told me that his father had been drinking and was weaving all over the road while driving him to his soccer game. When I talked to my husband about his arrest, my husband said that it had all been a mistake and that his lawyer was going to get him off, so there was no problem.

Now, I am concerned about the safety of my son when he is with his father. I don't want to send my son into that situation anymore. What can I do?

ANSWER: Run, don't walk, to your attorney and try to get an emergency order which stops your husband from having custody of your son. Your son is in danger when he is at your husband's house because your husband cannot control his drinking and lies about it, and because your husband places your son in danger by drinking and driving with him in the car. In short, your husband is an unfit parent because he has serious substance abuse issues and cannot care for your son properly.

You need to go back to court and change the court order so that your husband only has supervised visitation with your son. Your husband cannot be trusted to care for the child without someone else present to ride herd on the situation. Perhaps one of your husband's parents or other family member would be willing to supervise your husband and the child for a few hours every week.

Additionally, you need to get your son into counseling right away because children of alcoholics can carry a lot of emotional baggage. It could be of some considerable help to your son to have someone with whom he could talk about all of the problems and conflicts facing him as he grows up in a situation in which separation and substance abuse are major factors.

Don't delay and definitely don't believe the promises and statements that your husband makes about his drinking. Get the emergency court order that stops your husband from having custody of your son and make it your number one priority to protect your son from your husband's dangerous addiction.

# ONE YEAR TO FREEDOM

### March 1

My wife is from Otway, and so, it is no surprise that she loves drinking and fighting better than Peter loved the Lord.

When I married her, I had no idea of how tough a 5' 3", 120 pound woman could be, but I soon found out.

Things would go along OK so long as my wife had her way. But cross her, and my Lord honey, look out!

The first time that I put my foot down and said no to her was on July 4, 2006 after we had been drinking a few beers together. The words were no sooner out of my mouth when she went after me with a business end of a butcher knife. She only grazed my arm, and it didn't bleed very much, so I thought at the time that she really didn't mean it. Boy, was I wrong!

The second time that my wife came after me with that same butcher knife was on Halloween night in 2006. She had more beer to drink than I did so I could out run her, but it was a close thing. I left our house in a hurry and stayed away for a couple of months until she calmed down.

We got back together, but I later found out that during the time that she was cooling off with me, she was heating things up considerable with another man who turned out to be my cousin. Since her cattin' around had happened during our separation and it was just family involved, I was willing to overlook this little side trip of hers. However, she apparently kept up with my cousin after we got back together, and she thought that I wouldn't find out about him.

Well, secrets like that are not very long-lived in Otway, and my uncle told me all about it. While my wife was at work on February 14, 2007, I decided to give my wife a little Valentine's Day present. So I packed up my dog, wide screen TV, riding lawn mower, pickup truck, beer, and the butcher knife and moved out. I also beat the hell out of my cousin because he sure had it coming, but I left my wife alone because I sort of thought that she would wear me out or kill me if it was just me against her.

I want to get shed of my wife and get divorced from her as soon as possible because I have been mommicked long enough by this woman. Since I have to be separated from my wife for one year before I can file for a divorce, I want to use our first date of separation of Halloween, 2006 in counting out the year instead of February 14, 2007. We only were back together for about a month and my wife was cheating on me the whole time, so I figure that we weren't really living together as a husband and wife.

Can I use the first date I left home on Halloween, 2006 instead of the second date of February 14, 2007 as my date of separation?

ANSWER: If you moved back in with your wife, had sex with her, paid bills with her, kept up the house with her, and people thought that you were back together, then, you have resumed the marital relationship with your wife even though you were only together for a month or so. It also doesn't matter that she was stepping out with your cousin during that month because her adultery doesn't stop the clock as far as you both resuming your marital relationship.

Given that, you must use the date of February 14, 2007 which is when you last left your wife and not the first date when she ran you out of the house on Halloween, 2006 with a butcher knife in her hand.

So, you need to sit tight, stay away from your wife and cousin, and let time pass by. On February 15, 2008, you can file for a divorce, and then, you will soon be free of your wife who sounds like she really doesn't need a costume on Halloween.

# WHO'S THE DADDY?

### March 8

When my wife started losing weight, bought new black lingerie, and told me that she was visiting a friend in the hospital several evenings a week after work, I should have figured it out, but I didn't. No, I just stuck my head in the sand and wouldn't think about it at all.

Just when her "visiting" was happening four and five nights a week, my wife left me and would not tell me why. Nine months later, my wife gave birth to a baby boy who was cute as he could be with black, curly hair, dark brown eyes, a very full nose, and dark brown skin. The only problem with how the baby looked is that both my wife and I have blue eyes, fair skin, and blonde hair.

However, my wife swore up one side and down the other that this baby was my son and that the reason that he was a little dark and looked nothing like me was that there was some Cherokee Indian blood in her family. When I told my family what my wife had said and that I wanted to believe her, they all laughed at me.

I then hired a private investigator who followed my wife for several evenings. The PI later showed me the video tape of my wife meeting and going out with an Afer apartment where they spent most every night together. When I confronted my wife with this evidence, she said that they were just friends and that this man was out of work, and on some nights, he needed a free place to stay.

So, I told my wife that I wanted to have a paternity test done on her, me, and the baby to see if I was the father. My wife refused and instead, filed a law suit against me to get custody of the child and to make me pay child support to her. She says that the child was born while we were married so that makes him my son and that I have to support him until he graduates from high school. I make a good living as an owner of a construction business and she makes next to nothing as a part-time artist, so I would be paying her big bucks every month in child support.

If the child is mine, I will support him, but I do not think that he is my child because the child does not look anything like me and looks a whole lot like the African-American man whom my wife is providing a free place to stay overnight.

My wife is determined that I pay child support to her, and she is adamant that she will not have a test done to determine the paternity of this child. Is there a way out of this mess?

ANSWER: There is a way out but it will not be easy. North Carolina law says that a child born during a marriage is presumed to be the child of the husband. However, the law also says that the husband has the right to prove that he is not the father if there are pronounced racial differences between the mother, the husband, and the child.

In your case, you clearly have the right to ask the Court for a paternity test because the child appears to be racially different from you and your wife. You need to hire an attorney who should ask the Court to order that you, your wife, and the baby have a paternity test done. In this way, you will find out whether the reason for the child's dark features is his alleged Cherokee Indian ancestry or the fact that your wife committed adultery during your marriage with an African American man.

Once the paternity test is completed and the results known, I suspect that you will not be the child support gravy train that your wife had envisioned. However, it would be a good thing if you said a prayer for that child from time to time because he is going to need all the help that he can get. While the court will not require it of you if you are not the father, a little compassion and some financial help for this child would go a long way, and I recommend that you do just that for this unfortunate child.

# STUDMAN AND AN EXPECTATION OF PRIVACY

**March 15**

Last year, my wife of 10 years had been acting very strange. It started when she got a P.O. Box and had all of her mail sent there. Next, she joined a gym and got very buff and bought a lot of new, tight, low cut clothes to wear to her business meetings which increasing occurred late into the evening. Then came the implants and a cell phone in her name alone. Finally, she started spending a lot of time on her lap top computer when she was home at night and having precious little to do with me at any time.

When I asked her if anything was going on, my wife just flew off the handle and said that she was finding herself and to not bug her anymore about it. So, I decided to snoop around her stuff and see what I could see.

I looked in her purses and her car and found nothing, but when I looked in her brief case, I hit the motherload. I went through her day planner and found a date, October 15, 2006, with a red heart drawn around it and the words "Studman!!!" printed next to that date. That concerned me because I can't remember anything that happened on October 15 , 2006, and while my wife has called me a number of things over the years, she has never called me "Studman" and probably wouldn't put exclamation marks after that name if she did.

I then tried to get into her computer but I couldn't because I did not know her password. Suddenly, a lightening bolt of inspiration hit me! I typed in the password "Studman!!!", and open sesame, I was into her emails.

These emails confirmed my suspicions that my wife was having an affair with a man at her work because their emails were numerous and graphic. Some of the emails contained photographs of parts of my wife's anatomy which I had never seen before.

So, I printed out all of the emails and photographs. While my wife was at one of her late night "business meetings", I taped the photos all over the foyer of our house and sat down in the living room and waited for her to come home.

When my wife came through the door at 10:00 p.m., those pictures certainly stopped her in her tracks. She usually has a big mouth, but she was speechless. I told her that I knew all about her affair, that the marriage was over, that she would give me the house and my retirement, that she could take her clothes and her car, and that if she didn't agree and sign the necessary papers, I would take her to court and use these photographs as evidence.

My wife started to cry, turned around, ran out the door, and hasn't come back since. My lawyer has drawn up a separation agreement with the terms that I wanted. My wife has said that she will sign these papers but she hasn't yet, and I feel that she is dragging her feet. If I have to take her to court, can I use the emails and the photographs that I found on her computer as evidence of her adultery?

ANSWER: You cannot use your wife's Studman emails and photographs if she had an expectation of privacy with regard to these emails and photographs. Since she had her own computer rather than a computer used by the family and since she had a password which she did not tell you about, your wife very likely did have an expectation of privacy about her emails and photographs. Consequently, you probably will not be able to use her emails and photographs because you obtained this information by questionable means.

You need to talk to your attorney right away about how you got your wife's emails and photographs so that this evidence doesn't wind up hurting you instead of your wife. Even if you have to sweeten the equitable distribution pot for her a little bit, it would be worth it just to get the Separation Agreement signed and to not have to deal with questionable evidence in court.

Adultery is not a factor which North Carolina courts can consider in equitable distribution. So, don't let your anger and hurt stop you from accepting an advantageous settlement that you probably would not get in court.

# CAST AWAY

## March 22

My husband is a sot! Every day when he gets home from work, he starts drinking gin, and every time he looks at me, he has another big one. He just aggravates the fool out of me.

The last straw happened one night when he had drunk four or five gin and tonics and decided that he was going to get the cast net out. Somehow, he found the cast net and staggered out to the dock. While on the dock, he rared back and threw the cast net forward as hard as he could. The only problem was that he forgot to let go of the cast net and sailed off head first into Core Sound along with the cast net.

At the time, I was in the house, and I heard him start to cuss up a blue fogged storm and holler for me to come help him. I came out and saw him floundering around in the water just off the dock. When I went on the dock and leaned my hand over to help him up, my husband grabbed my hand and pulled me into the water with him. Of course, he thought that was funny.

When I stood there in the water soaking wet, I told him that I was through with him and that he would have to move out. While he has tried to sweet talk me some since then, I have not changed my mind.

The problem is that my husband will not move out of the house even though I ask him every day to do so. I have decided that I am going to have the locks to the house changed while he is at work, and then, I will put all of his things in boxes on the front porch. So, he will not be able to get back into the house and will have to take his stuff and go elsewhere and I will finally have some peace and quiet. Is this a good idea?

ANSWER: Throwing your husband and his stuff out the door in this manner is not a good idea. You cannot just change the locks on the house and keep your husband out because you want him gone. Unhappily for him, he has a legal right to live in this house with you because he is your husband and this is where he lives. You also cannot put his stuff on the porch because he has a right to keep his things in his residence.

If you do put his things on the porch and they are stolen or damaged by the weather, a court could hold you responsible for replacing them. So, you should sit tight and leave his stuff alone.

Since you have decided that the marriage is over, you need to talk to a family law attorney about other ways to resolve the ending of your marriage. It is possible that you can legally get possession of the house through a law suit with claims for a divorce from bed and board and alimony. A family law attorney can advise you whether or not this is a possibility in your case.

Don't let anger and spite guide you as you go down the path to separation. Take the high road and hope that your husband will do the same.

# WHEN "MINE! MINE! MINE!" IS OURS

## March 29

When my wife told me that she was leaving me, I told her "Hurrah! Good riddance!" I was glad because she has never done anything for me. All the 31 years of our marriage, I worked hard while she stayed home and never worked. She just ate bons bons, watched TV, raised our five kids, and kept the house. She never earned one thin dime!

When my wife told me that she wanted one-half of everything we now have, I told her "No way! Tough luck!"

I was the one who worked all the time during the marriage – not her! Throughout the marriage, all the money from my pay checks went into a bank account in my name alone, and I gave my wife a weekly allowance for groceries.

I did all the work! I paid all the bills! With my money, I paid for a house, two cars, a big stock portfolio, a 401(k), and several large certificates of deposit. These things are all in my name alone, and they all belong solely to me. I paid for them, and they are mine!

I told my wife that she could have the older car and the furniture from the guest bedroom that her Aunt

Mildred gave her, but that was it. I said to her that if she wanted more things, she would just have to get a job and work hard like I did and use her own money to pay for new stuff.

She started to cry and said that she was going to see a lawyer. I just laughed at her and said "That won't make any difference!"

I feel certain that I am right, but I just want to make sure that my house, my cars, and my financial investments are all mine because I paid for them during the marriage with my earnings, and they are all titled in my name alone.

ANSWER: I hope that you are sitting down when you read this column because you are in for one big, unpleasant, and well-deserved surprise.

In North Carolina, all of the marital assets accumulated during the marriage from money earned during the marriage by either spouse are marital property. Consequently, each spouse is entitled to one-half of the net marital assets. It does not matter how these assets are titled if these assets were paid for by a spouse's employment earnings during the marriage.

So, your wife is entitled to one-half of the net marital assets paid for by your employment earnings during the marriage. You cannot avoid your wife's right to one-half of the net value of the house, the two cars, the stock portfolio, the 401(k), and the certificates of deposit by putting these assets in your name alone.

As a result, you need to be prepared to suck it up and fork over one-half of the net value of these marital assets to your wife. To do otherwise would not be fair, but it's my guess that you are not overly concerned with being fair to your wife.

Since your wife will probably make good on her threat to see an attorney, you need to do the same as soon as possible.  If you think that your wife's attorney won't be able to make a difference in the present situation, just you wait and see.

If you continue to be greedy, selfish, and mean to your wife, all kinds of surprises await you in court in the fairly foreseeable future.  My guess is that these surprises will be mostly unpleasant and that you will deserve every one of them.

So, divide the marital assets and marital debts equally with your wife.  Stop bellowing "Mine!  Mine!  Mine!" and be fair to your wife.

# BIGAMY AT THE BEACH

**April 5**

When Hurricane Fran was coming, I told my husband, Bubba, that we have got to get out of our house since it was a single wide trailer on a canal by the ocean and only about five feet above sea level. Bubba, who is stubborn as a mule but not as smart, said that no storm was going to run him out of his house and that he was staying. I told Bubba, "OK, you can do that if you want to, but I am out of here." So, I packed up my car with all of my stuff that I cared about and went to stay in Raleigh with my aunt and uncle.

Well, Hurricane Fran came ashore, and Bubba sat in his barcolounger and just started drinking hard. As the water began to come into our trailer, he put on a life jacket and sort of floated around the living room for a while. After several more beers, he decided that he had to abandon ship because the water was then getting close to ceiling. So, he busted out a window, crawled out of it, climbed up on the top of trailer, and held on for dear life during the rest of the storm.

God must protect fools because Bubba survived his own stupidity and ended up perched on what was left of our trailer about two blocks from our original lot. Pretty much everything we owned was destroyed, and we didn't have any flood insurance because Bubba had said that it was too expensive and he wouldn't pay for it.

With no home to go back to, I stayed in Raleigh, got a job, and ended up meeting someone else, so I never went back to Bubba. Bubba got another old trailer and put it on poles about ten feet in the air. As for me, I was very happy with my new job and my new flame in Raleigh.

Time went by. It has now been over ten years since I left Bubba. Last year, I got married to my flame but I never divorced Bubba since I figured that seven years had gone by and I assumed that we had a common law divorce. I am now pregnant, and my new husband is very happy about it. I just wanted to make sure that I have a common law divorce and that everything is OK.

ANSWER: You may have been smart about hurricanes, but you have made several big mistakes in your assumptions regarding divorce and remarriage. In North Carolina, there is no such thing as common law divorce.

It doesn't matter how long you have been separated from Bubba. If you have not filed in court for a divorce and have not received a divorce judgment from the court, you are still married to Bubba. Time going by doesn't entitle you to anything except trouble if you don't file and receive a divorce through the court.

However, there is such a thing as bigamy, which is a felony in North Carolina, and right now, you are a bigamist. If anyone wanted to press the issue, you could be charged with bigamy, and then, you would be in an even bigger scrape.

The upshot of this whole thing is that you are still married to Bubba, and you are not legally married to The Flame. The marriage to The Flame is void because you still have a husband, Bubba, who is alive and well and living ten feet in the air at the beach.

As you might expect, void marriages cause a lot of problems. For example, you do not have any rights as a married person in your relationship with The Flame. Your rights to things such as social security benefits, inheritance, equitable distribution, and alimony, are non-existent because you are not the legal wife of The Flame.

Well, you have got yourself into a mess, but there is a way out of it. Get a family law attorney to get you divorced from Bubba as soon as possible. You also need to have a very painful conversation with The Flame about this whole situation and inform him that you and he need to get married again. With a baby on the way, I would say that time is of the essence.

After the divorce from Bubba is final, a quick and quiet marriage to The Flame at a magistrate's office would make you the legal wife of The Flame. Hopefully, The Flame is still happy that he married you the first time and will agree to marry you one more time.

Don't ignore this situation since it will only get worse and more complicated as time goes by. You also owe it to your unborn child to try and get your marital status resolved before he or she is born. In the future, don't assume anything regarding divorce and marriage because it could cost you more than you could ever imagine.

# COURT ORDERS CAN'T COERCE
# A DAUGHTER'S LOVE

## April 12

After 15 years of marriage and one child, my sorry excuse of a husband left me for his secretary who was twenty years younger than him. At first, I was really upset because I thought at the time that even a bad husband was better than no husband at all. However as time went on, I realized that my life was a lot better without him since I did not have to deal with his bad moods, unfaithful behavior, and his annoying habit of noisily sucking his teeth. Whenever I thought about how my married life had been, I felt like sending the secretary-girl friend a thank you note.

Unfortunately, our daughter, who is 13, is not having an easy time of it since the separation. In a court order, my husband and I had agreed that our daughter would spend every other weekend and two weeks in the summer with him.

Recently, my daughter does not want to go and visit with her father because he lives in a one bedroom apartment which is filthy, and my daughter has to sleep on a saggy couch in the living room. My husband also spends a lot of time on these weekends with his girl friend who is included in all the activities that my husband does with my daughter. As a result, my daughter feels like a fifth wheel and feels ignored by her father.

To put icing and pink sugar on the cake, my husband has now filed for divorce, and I was served last week. Over this last weekend, he announced to my daughter that he is getting married to the girl friend in June and expects her to be in his wedding party as a bridesmaid. My daughter went ballistic and told him in no uncertain terms that she does not like his girl friend, does not like him, does not want to be the bitch's (her term, not mine) bridesmaid, will not go to the wedding, and will not go back to his stinking apartment ever again for visitation.

In response, my husband yelled at her that she would come for visitation with him as ordered by the court and his wedding or else he would have me held in contempt by the court and put in jail. My daughter burst into tears and yelled back at him that if he did any such thing to me, she would hate him for the rest of her life. She then packed her stuff up, headed out the door, and walked five miles home.

I was very surprised to see her at the door. When I heard her story, I told her that she could see her father if she wanted to but that I was not going to make her go if she refused to do so. I called her father up, and he screamed and yelled that if I did not make our daughter come to see him on his weekends for visitation and go to his wedding, he was going to haul me back into court and have the court hold me in contempt for not making our daughter see him during those times.

Now, I have always encouraged my daughter to see her father and have never tried to prevent her from having a good relationship with him. However, I am not going to force her to go and see him if she does not want to go. In fact, I cannot make her go if she does not want to do so. She is as tall as I am, and I am not going to get into a physical confrontation with her to make her see her father.

Can I be held in contempt by the court if I do not force my daughter to see her father on his weekends and participate in his wedding?

ANSWER: If you have not undermined your husband's relationship with your daughter and have actively encouraged your daughter to have visitation with your husband, you cannot be held in contempt by the court because your daughter refuses to see your husband for his court-ordered visitation. Further, the court order does not require your daughter to participate in your husband's wedding, so you cannot be held in contempt if your daughter refuses to walk down the aisle flinging rose petals or whatever other role your husband may have in mind for your daughter at his wedding.

You should probably see a family law attorney to ensure that you are doing all of right things and none of the wrong ones and to prepare to meet any legal challenge that your husband may want to throw up at you in order to get his way.

Additionally, you, your husband, and your daughter need to see a family counselor right away. This counselor needs to talk to everyone and make recommendations about your daughter's visitation with your husband and help him understand how he has undermined his daughter's love for him by his bad behavior towards her and you. Your daughter also needs help in dealing with your separation, divorce, her father's wedding, and his new girlfriend/wife.

For better or worse, you all need to understand that you, your husband, and your daughter are still a family even though you and your husband are not living together and will shortly be divorced. Your husband needs to understand that a court order cannot make his daughter love him and want to see him and that if he wants to have the love of his daughter, he needs to treat her with love and respect.

# WHAT YOU SEE IS WHAT YOU GET

### April 19

I have had this on and off thing going with this man for over six years. It was always "Can't live with him and can't live without him." I wanted to get married and have kids, and he wanted to drink, chase women, and do what he wanted to do when he wanted to do it. So, I put up with his bad behavior for years because I thought that I loved him and could change the way he was.

Well, I finally wore him down, and he agreed to marry me. He wouldn't agree to a church wedding or a reception or a honeymoon, and he wouldn't wear a wedding ring either, but he agreed to marry me at the magistrates office. So, I agreed to all of his conditions, and off we went.

At the magistrates' office, I began to get cold feet. I mean there I was in jeans with no flowers, no bridesmaids, no church wedding, no reception, none of my family and friends present, and no honeymoon. I started to tell my boy friend that we should just call it off when he began to yell that if I didn't marry him then and there, he would never marry me later on. So, I went through with the civil ceremony, but I knew at the time that I was making a terrible and stupid mistake.

After the wedding, I started to drive us back to his apartment. On the way, I wrecked the car and totaled it. No one was hurt, but it was an omen.

That night, my husband went out and got Chinese carryout for dinner to celebrate. As I looked at my won ton soup in its plastic container, I thought that the writing was on the wall for this marriage.

But the wedding night was pretty good, and my husband was very passionate, and I thought that maybe being married to him might not be so bad.

Two nights later, my husband didn't come home after work and stayed out all night. I was worried sick and tried to reach him on his cell phone, but he didn't answer my calls. I was just about to call the police when he rolled in at 7:00 a.m. the next morning with love bites (not mine) on his neck and looking like he had been rode hard and put to bed wet. When I asked him where he had been, he said that it was none of my business and that I had just better get used to his being gone from time to time if I wanted to be married to him.

I waited until he left for work, and then, I packed up all my stuff and moved out. That was over two weeks ago, and I still haven't heard from him even though he knows how to get up with me.

So, I want to get my marriage annulled since it only lasted three days which is really kind of a long date rather than a marriage. Can I get this marriage annulled?

ANSWER: Unfortunately, your marriage cannot be annulled based on the fact that it only lasted a few days. If you and your husband were single when you married each other, were properly married, knew what you were doing when you got married, and were able to have sexual intercourse, you cannot get an annulment unless your husband was your uncle or brother or unless you were double first cousins. I can only hope that is not the case.

Being married for a very short time doesn't entitle you to anything except a broken heart and a divorce. There are no annulments in North Carolina for bad judgment and marriages of brief duration.

So, you need to sit tight for one year from the date that you walked out the door on your marriage. After that one year anniversary, you can file for divorce in North Carolina but not before.

A good lesson to learn from this is that you can't change a person's behavior before and after marriage. What you see is what you get, especially after marriage.

# WHAT IS IN THE BEST INTERESTS OF THE CHILD?

**April 26**

Until recently, I was in a very intense, live-in lesbian relationship which resulted in the birth of a child. My former girl friend and I met each other five years ago. After a year of dating, we had a very beautiful commitment ceremony (because we could not get married to each other in North Carolina), and I moved into her house.

Two years later, we decided that we wanted to have a child and agreed that I would be the one to have the baby since I was younger and in better health. As for the father, we listed the physical characteristics that we wanted and placed our order for that type of sperm donor at the in-vitro fertilization clinic.

We wanted to use in-vitro fertilization rather than a "quickie" with some "wham bam thank you ma'm" man because we wanted to control the father's gene pool as much as possible, we didn't want me to have sex with a man, and we wanted the father to be an anonymous sperm donor so that he would not be present in the child's life and cause us problems.

So, my ex-girlfriend was present while I was artificially inseminated at this clinic, and she went with me to all of my pre-natal doctor visits and my birth classes. She was also with me during my whole labor and delivery and cut the umbilical cord of the baby who turned out to be a little boy.

At first, things between my former girlfriend, me, and the baby were fine. My girlfriend and I signed a parenting agreement which stated that we were going to co-parent this baby and share the responsibility of raising him, but I was the one who stayed home and cared for him most of the time. When my son started to talk, he called me "Mama" and my former girlfriend "Mawmee", and we told him that he was very lucky because he had two mommies while most children only had one.

Then, I met Dick.

I was out playing in the park with my son when Dick came by walking his new puppy. My son started playing with the puppy and I started talking to Dick. Dick's and my attraction to each other was immediate and over-powering.

We kept meeting each other at the park until one thing led to another, and I ended up in bed with Dick. After three torrid and passionate months, I told Dick everything about my then girlfriend, and he asked me to leave my girlfriend and move in with him.

So, one day when my girlfriend was at work, I packed up some things and my son and moved out of her house and moved in with Dick so that I could avoid a confrontation with my girlfriend with my son present. I left her a "Dear Joan" letter explaining some of the reasons why I had left but I didn't tell her about Dick.

After a month, I thought that everything was going

to be fine. Dick and I were very happy together, my son was calling him "Daddy", and I hadn't heard too much from my former girlfriend who only saw my son a few times for a couple of hours during that month.

Then, a deputy sheriff came to the door and served me with a law suit from my former girlfriend who is asking for shared physical and legal custody of my son. I am really upset because I don't want her to continue to be involved with me and my son. I want to get married and have Dick adopt my son, and I don't want my son to find out later on about my wild fling into lesbian land.

Can my former girlfriend get shared legal and physical custody of my son? How can I stop her from ruining my life and the life of my son?


ANSWER: The short answer is that it is not clear whether or not your former girlfriend has a right to have custody or visitation with your son because the North Carolina Court of Appeals and the North Carolina Supreme Court have not made a decision regarding whether or not a partner, who is not the biological parent in a same-sex relationship, has any rights to the child born to the other partner in that same-sex relationship. Three cases are now before the North Carolina Court of Appeals, so their decisions should come out within a year.

Now, here is the long answer. You need to find a family law attorney who will quickly respond to your former girlfriend's law suit. The first thing to look at is whether your former girlfriend has something called "standing". A non-parent, third party like your girlfriend could only have standing if she had a parent-like relationship with your son.  Of course, she will argue that she has acted like a parent while you will have to argue otherwise.

If the court decides that she does not have standing, her claims are dismissed, and you go home happy. However if the court decides that she does have standing, the court will next have to decide whether you are an unfit mother or have acted in a manner inconsistent with your protected status as a parent.

The Court will look at things such as her participation in your impregnation, pregnancy, and child birth, and in the child's life.  The Court will also look at your signing the parenting agreement which is not a legally binding document, but which may give direction to the Court as to whether you voluntarily gave up some of your parental rights regarding your son to your former girlfriend.

If the Court finds that you are not an unfit mother or that you did not act in a manner inconsistent with your protected status as a parent, you win and your girlfriend has no rights to your son.  If the Court finds otherwise, the next step in the process is that the Court has to determine what kind of custody and visitation with you and your former girlfriend is in the best interests of your child.  The Court could then order that your former girlfriend does get to have shared physical and legal custody of your son if the Court decides that it is in the best interest of your son.

So, you need to get ready for the fight of your life. Get going and hire an attorney because the outcome of your case is not at all clear.

If you decide to get pregnant in the future, you might think about the child's needs first rather than what you want. You might think about how a child feels being raised intentionally without a father or without the benefit of the parents' marriage and how that child will be viewed by other children and their parents in your community. You would do well to think of what is best for the child instead of what is best for you.

# READ THE FINE PRINT -
# THE DEVIL IS IN THE DETAIL!

## MAY 3

When I first met her, I thought that true love had finally come to me.  She was beautiful, intelligent, really built, and twenty years younger than me.  When she agreed to marry me, I couldn't believe my good luck.

After we got married, she moved into my house which I had owned in my name alone for many years.  My house was on the ocean in Pine Knoll Shores and had a great view, so it was worth a pretty penny.  By working hard, I had paid off the mortgage early, and so, I didn't owe a dime on it when we got married.

We had only been married a few months when my wife told me that she wanted to redo the kitchen and the bathrooms which were admittedly a little outdated.  So, I got a mortgage loan in both of our names for $75,000.00 from my bank with my house as the collateral.

Unbeknownst to me at the closing, the closing attorney redid the deed to my house such that the new deed changed the ownership of my house from me as sole owner to my wife and me as owners as husband and wife.  We all signed this new deed and all the papers for the new mortgage which was in both of our names.

Blissfully ignorant of what I had given up and given away to my new wife, I hired a contractor to start the renovation. When the renovation was about half way completed, I came home unexpectedly early one after-noon and found my wife in bed with the contractor. It was not a pretty sight.

I grabbed a crow bar and chased him out of my house. He was buck naked and barefooted but ran surprisingly fast and I couldn't catch him though I tried for several blocks.

When I came back home, my wife was packing her bags, and she left without either of us saying much of anything. After she left, I thought that I was done with her because the marriage had only lasted four months.

However, my wife quickly filed for equitable distri-bution and claimed that she was now entitled to one-half of the value of my ocean front house because I had deeded it to her and me as husband and wife.

I can't believe that I have to give one-half of the value of this house to that lying, cheating, sorry, no-good wife of mine. What's the deal? Does she actually get to keep one-half of the value of my house when I would have to sell my house to pay her that amount?

ANSWER: Unfortunately for you, the law is very clear that you have made a marital gift to your wife of one-half of the value of the house when you deeded the house from yourself to both you and her as husband and wife (tenants by the entireties). Now, she is an equal co-owner of the house and is entitled to ask the Court to grant her the one-half value of the house in equitable distribution.

However, you are entitled to ask the Court for an unequal distribution of the marital assets in your favor because you have contributed a substantial separate asset, the house, to the marital estate.

The Court is not supposed to consider marital misconduct in equitable distribution. Nonetheless, the facts in your case, which include the very short duration of the marriage, the fact that you did not know that you were transferring the deed from you alone to you and your wife, and the bad conduct of your wife, may sway the Court to grant you an unequal distribution largely in your favor. There is no way to tell how it all will go until you get in court.

So, the moral of this story is to not be hoodwinked by youth and beauty and to always check the deed to your house before you sign it to make sure that you are not giving away more than what you had planned.

# PAYING FOR THE FREE RIDE

**May 10**

My husband and I were married for eleven years and had five kids before he left me for our twenty year old baby-sitter. I think that I miss my baby-sitter more than him. At least I am no longer a frequent flyer at my obstetrician's office.

So, he left and didn't help me out much with the kids because he was spending all his money on alcohol, drugs, and hootchie koochie. Since he spent a lot of time being hung over or under the influence, he never could keep a job very long, and it was hard to get child support from him.

Finally, he got a job as a caretaker for an estate with a big house owned by some people from Off. My ex-husband now has it made in the shade because he has a free caretaker's house to live in and a free truck to drive as part of his employment. Also, these people are from Raleigh and only show up one or two weekends a month, so he can stay drunk most of the month and still get paid.

Recently, I have been trying to get child support from him through Carteret County Child Support Enforcement, and they are trying to figure out his income.

He has repeatedly told me that he only makes $7.00 per hour for a 40 hour week and that he should only pay me child support based on that income.

Child Support Enforcement has told me that they can include the values of the monthly rental of the house and the truck as income to my ex-husband because they are in-kind payments received by my ex-husband as part of his employment, and these in-kind payments, such as the free rental house and truck to drive, amount to a lot of money and reduce his personal living expenses.

Meanwhile, my ex-husband is hollering (in a slurred sort of way) that he only earns $280.00 per week in cash money, and that amount is what should be used to calculate his child support. Who is right?

ANSWER: Who do you think you should believe? A drunk who abandons his children and won't support them or Carteret County Child Support Enforcement?

North Carolina law is very clear and say that "Expense reimbursements or in-kind payments (for example, the use of a company car, free housing, or reimbursed meals) received by a parent in the course of employment, self-employment, or operation of a business are counted as income if they are significant and reduce personal living expenses."

Here, your ex-husband has free housing and a free truck to use, so the monthly rental value of the house and the truck needs to be calculated and added to his monthly income in order to determine his child support obligation. I am sure that he won't like it, but that is the way it is, so he can get pleased or displeased.

Ask a local real estate company to give you an estimate of what the monthly rent on your ex-husband's house should be and ask a car rental agency what the monthly rental cost would be on your husband's free truck. If they will give you these values in writing, give them to Child Support Enforcement so they can use these figures in calculating his monthly income.

Tell your ex-husband that he is finally going to pay child support to you based on his complete income and that his free ride is over.

# BAD ACTIONS NEED TO HAVE BAD CONSEQUENCES

**May 17**

I am writing because I am very afraid and don't know what to do. There is this weird guy in one of my classes at Carteret Community College, and he has decided that he is in love with me and wants me to go out with him.

It started out with him sitting next to me all the time in class and repeatedly asking me out. He would look at me so strangely, that it scared me and I told him every time that I would not go out on a date with him. I thought that would be the end of it, but he just went to the next level. Somehow, he found out my class schedule and would follow me from class to class and to my car at the end of the day. He would try to hand me presents and talk to me, but I just ignored him.

Then, he started calling me at my home and doing hang-ups at strange hours of the night. I have caller ID, and all these weird calls in the middle of the night were from him. Occasionally, he would leave messages on my answering machine, and these messages would say that he would always love me and that he knew where I was all the time, and that some day, I would be his forever.

He also started leaving notes on the windshield of my car so that just about every morning, there was a love note from him stuck under the wiper blade. His letters are just nuts because he has this whole fantasy that I also love him, and he writes me about what he would like to do in bed with me.

Recently, I was in the grocery store, and I felt someone brush by and rub my backside as he went by. It was him, and he was standing nearby smiling with this deranged look on his face. That was the last straw. I yelled at him to get his crazy ass away from me and to leave me alone. All of a sudden, he became enraged and got in my face and yelled at me that if I didn't love him back, I would be really sorry.

At that point, I ran out of the store, jumped in my car, and went home. I am really afraid of this man. What can I do to protect myself?

ANSWER: You need to be very careful because you are in a dangerous situation. This man is probably crazy, and crazy people often do not have any limits on what they will or will not do.

So, you need to load this bad boy up with every criminal and civil remedy you are entitled to use.

First, you need to file criminal charges against him for stalking, harassing phone calls, and assault on a female. Ask the magistrate to order that as a condition of his bond, he is to stay away from you and have no contact with you. If he violates these conditions, immediately contact the district attorney's office and try to get him put in jail until his trial.

You also need to send him a letter telling him to stay away from the property where you live and you need to let him know that if he comes onto your property, you will charge him with criminal trespass. If he then shows up at your house, you immediately need to file this additional criminal charge of trespass against him. The idea is to criminally charge him with as much as possible so that his actions have consequences that he doesn't like i.e., the criminal court experience and jail time.

Additionally, you need to hire an attorney to file a civil law suit against him, and this law suit needs to ask the court to order that this man have no contact with you. No contact means that he cannot visit, assault, molest, interfere, stalk, abuse, injure, or contact you by telephone, written communication, or electronic means. It also means that he cannot come to your residence, school, place of employment or other specified places at times when you are present such as church services.

Further, you need to contact the administration of Carteret Community College about the problems that you are having with this man. If he is not a student, the school could ban him from the campus. If he is a student, the school could explain to him that if he wants to continue being a student, he immediately needs to leave you completely alone.

Finally, you need to realize that criminal charges and restraining orders are ultimately just pieces of paper and that if a man has serious mental health issues, these pieces of paper may not stop him from hurting or killing you.

You need to carry a cell phone with you at all times and immediately call 911 if you see him. You might think about carrying pepper spray or Mace, but be aware that these sprays will do you no good if you hesitate to use them since he could take these things away from you and use them against you.

As for carrying a knife or a gun, these items may afford you more protection if you know how to use them and if you are willing to do so, but they may put you in more danger if you don't know what you are doing and are reluctant to use them. Additionally, you need to have a concealed carry permit for a concealed handgun outside of your home, so you would need to pass the background security check as well as the classes and firearm training to get this permit.

You are now in a dangerous situation and need to take action quickly. His actions towards you need to have some very negative consequences. If you can put him in jail for even a little while, do it. Wearing orange for just a few days can often be a very effective anger management program.

Don't think that this situation will get any better on its own because it will very likely get a whole lot worse without you doing the things outlined above to stop him. Don't delay because your life could be at risk.

# SEX, LIES, AND BOGUS DOMESTIC VIOLENCE

**May 24**

During the last six months, my wife's behavior towards me changed dramatically. Before, she was a tigress in bed, but later, she just didn't want to have anything to do with me. She also lost 20 pounds and started wearing these hot, short skirts, but she didn't like it when I told her how great she looked.

Last week, she asked me to go out to dinner with her. So, we went to our favorite romantic restaurant. It had been a while since we had been there, and I was really hoping that she was going to tell me that she wanted to make our marriage work.

Almost as soon as we were seated, she instead told me that she was not happy in our marriage and wanted a divorce. Further, she wanted me to move out and leave her the house and the kids plus pay her alimony every month for years and years. I was completely taken off guard. It was a real kick in the head.

When I told her I wouldn't leave, she became very angry with me and said that she would get me out of the house one way or the other because she was going to live in that house, not me.

Now, my family gave me $35,000.00 to help buy our house, and I used that money as the down payment. Since I loved and trusted my wife, I put the house in both of our names.

My wife also said that she was going to have custody of our two children, boys ages 8 and 10, and that I could see them every other weekend and that was the way it was going to be. I told her that at a minimum, I wanted the boys one-half of the time. After I said that, she got red in the face and shouted at me that she was getting the house and the kids one way or the other and there wouldn't be anything that I could do about it. She also said that I was going to be very sorry that I wouldn't do things her way. Then, she got up and charged out of the restaurant.

The next day, my wife and I went to work, but I doubled back to our house and proceeded to go through her purses, her cell phone bills, her pants pockets, and her papers on her desk. I couldn't read her emails because she had changed her password, and I didn't know what it was.

Finally, I hit pay dirt. Behind the dryer in the laundry room, I found a packet of steamy, heavy-breathing letters to her from one of her male co-workers. In the letters, this guy told my wife how he loved her and what he was planning to do with her in bed the next time that they got together. I also realized that during the times that my wife had told me that she was visiting her sister she was in fact with this guy.

So, I waited. That evening after we put the kids in bed, I sat down in the living room next to my wife and showed her the letters that I had found. I asked her to stop seeing this man and to try and work things out with me.

Instead of being remorseful or in any way apologetic, my wife laughed at me and told me that I was moving out without the kids, that her boy friend was moving in this house with her and the kids, that her boy friend was much more of a man and better in bed than I was, that it was her life, and that I could not tell her what to do and how to act. She then screamed at me to get out of her house.

Stupidly, I lost my temper. As she tried to leave, I started to call her names and grabbed her arm. Laughing, she pulled herself away and said that she was now going to call 911 and get me out of the house legally because she was a victim of domestic violence.

She did call 911. The police came and arrested me for assault on a female and took me to jail. By the time that I got out of jail the next day, my wife had also filed a domestic violence complaint and got a judge to sign an Ex Parte Order which gave her temporary possession of the house and told me to stay out of the house and away from her. I was only allowed to go with a deputy to get some of my clothes and my toothbrush.

My wife also filed a complaint for custody, child support, post-separation support, alimony, and equitable distribution. She asked for sole custody of our children because she said that I was violent and that she was a victim of domestic violence. Since I am supposed to stay away from my wife, I have not been able to see my children, and she will not agree to my seeing them or even calling them on the phone.

I am dumbfounded. My wife had an affair, got caught, and has used a bunch of lies about domestic violence to get the legal system to kick me out of my house and keep my children away from me. What can I do?

ANSWER: Unfortunately, you have now learned one of the very important lessons of ending a marriage – Never, never, never touch or yell at a spouse once the marriage is coming apart. It is all too easy for a spouse to use the other spouse's fleeting out-of-control moment to file criminal charges and a domestic violence restraining order against the other spouse.

Often, a cheating spouse is very calculated in trying to get the other spouse to lose his or her temper and yell at and/or hit The Cheater because then, The Cheater can use the legal system's domestic violence provisions to get the house and the kids and to get the other spouse out the door at little cost to The Cheater. Often, the Cheater figures that the best defense is a good offense.

So, you fell into the trap. Now, you need a family law attorney right away to try and get the domestic violence restraining order dismissed and to file an answer and counterclaims to your wife's law suit for custody, child support, post-separation support, alimony, and equitable distribution. Your attorney also needs to address custody of the children and possession of the marital residence so that you are not shut out from your children and your home at the very start of this litigation.

This is all going to be horribly expensive, time-consuming, and upsetting. Do not have any conversations or any other communication of any type with your wife. All communication with your wife now needs to go through your attorney. You also probably need to hire a private investigator to document your wife's infidelities with her co-worker. Your attorney will help you orchestrate your defense to your wife's charges against you.

In the future, don't ever be alone with your wife even if the domestic violence restraining order is dismissed. Unfortunately, your wife is a cunning and conniving cheater who will stop at nothing in order to get her own way. You will always need to keep your temper and your guard up around her so that nothing like this will ever happen to you again.

# THE HIGH COST OF SPEEDING BULLETS

**May 31**

After going out with my boy friend for three years, he finally asked me to marry him last Christmas when we were in Atlantic Beach visiting my parents. He gave me a beautiful diamond engagement ring, and we set a wedding date for the first weekend in June this year. We planned to live in his apartment in Newport until we could buy a larger home after the wedding. I was so excited.

Since I am an only child and I have never been married before, my family and I went all out. We invited 250 guests on beautifully engraved invitations, reserved one of the big churches in Morehead City for the wedding and a first class hotel on the ocean at Pine Knoll Shores for the reception which included hors d'oeuvres, a sit-down dinner, and dancing with a live beach music band from Wilmington.

My mother and I flew to New York City and went shopping for my wedding dress, veil, and shoes and the bride's maids' dresses and shoes. Additionally, we ordered magnificent arrangements of flowers for the church and the reception, and lovely bouquets for me and my bridesmaids and corsages for my mother, my grandmothers and my fiance's mother and his grand-mothers.

I also paid for wedding announcements in the local and Raleigh newspapers and had engagement pictures taken. Last week, I also had my wedding photographs taken wearing my dress and veil and placed an order for these pictures.

Since my fiancé said that we were going on a two week honeymoon to Hawaii, I bought numerous new out-fits and sexy nightgowns so that our honeymoon would be even more memorable.

During the last several months, people have given me several showers where I received numerous expensive and wonderful gifts. Since I was registered at several upscale department stores, I also received many pres-ents in the mail from people who would not be able to attend the wedding. In fact, I have one whole room at my home full of these presents, and I had even started writing thank you notes for all of these gifts.

The wedding express was going full tilt and roar-ing along when two weeks before the wedding date, my fiancé came over one evening and told me that he was going to call off the wedding. He said that three months ago, he had started dating his old high school sweet heart, and that this week, he had decided that he wanted to marry her instead of me. He said that he hoped that I would understand and that she was the one that made him truly happy and not me. As sort of a postscript, he mumbled that he was sorry, and then, he walked out the door.

I was stunned. I couldn't believe what he had said to me. I called my mother, and we cried together for a long time.

The next day, I had to call every one of those 250 people on the wedding list and tell them that the wedding was off. I also had to call my bridesmaids, the church, the soloist, the organist, the hotel, the photographer, the cake maker, the band, the florist, and the hotel where all my out-of-town guests had made reservations. I even had to call my ex-fiancé's parents and groomsmen because my ex-fiancé did not have the guts to call them.

Just thinking about the room where all of our engagement and wedding presents are displayed is overwhelming. Now, I not only have to write a note of appreciation, but I have to return all of these presents to the people who sent them.

Of course, I have lost all of my deposits and may still have to pay full price for many of the wedding costs because I have had to cancel at the last minute. I am still negotiating with all these providers and am trying to work things out with them.

Needless to say, the expense of this non-wedding has been enormous. I have spent over $50,000.00 and had to take out a loan to pay for everything. My fiancé, who is a doctor and can well afford it, has refused to pay for even one-half of these costs. He said that it was my idea to have a big wedding, and so, while he is sorry that it was so expensive, he is not going to pay for it.

Not only am I emotionally wrecked by being dumped by my ex-fiancé but I am financially devastated as well. Is there any way that I can make my ex-fiancé pay for some if not all of these wedding costs?

ANSWER: Since you were engaged in North Carolina, planned to wed in North Carolina, and planned to have your marital residence in North Carolina, you have the right to file a law suit against your ex-fiancé in a North Carolina court for breach of promise to marry.

The right to sue for breach of promise to marry is not available in most states, but North Carolina does have this type of law suit. Through this suit, you can ask for damages for mental anguish, loss of expectations about wealth and social position, injury to reputation, and the actual expenses that you incurred for the wedding.

You must be able to prove that you and your boyfriend exchanged promises to marry each other and that the wedding was not called off due to any misbehavior on your part. You should also show evidence of the emotional trauma that you went through due to the wedding being called off by your ex-fiancé as well as evidence of your ex-fiancé's wealth and social position. Finally, you should gather up all of the receipts for all of the costs that you incurred for the wedding and ask the court to order that your ex-fiancé pay you for all of these costs.

So, you need to get all of this information together and find a good lawyer who will file suit for you against this faithless doctor. He needs to reap what he has sown and pay you a lot of money. Over time, you will hopefully also realize that a speeding bullet just passed you by when your cheating boy friend became your ex-fiancé rather than your husband.

# HOW TO EARN JEWELS IN YOUR CROWN IN HEAVEN

**June 7**

I just don't know what I am going to do about Mama. She is 92 years old, speaks her mind, but is really not quite with it.

Mama and Daddy never got along very well and spent a lot of time bickering with each other. Daddy would go off hunting, fishing, and drinking at the Banks a lot with his friends, and Mama was very involved with the church, so they managed to avoid each other a lot over the years.

Since Daddy died last month, Mama has perked right up. On numerous occasions when people have called on her to express their sympathy, she has told them that she is glad that Daddy was dead and that her only regret was that she didn't divorce him thirty years ago.

She then has gone on to say that she is finally going to sell their house, which Daddy had refused to sell because he didn't want to live anywhere else, and that she is going to move into a nearby assisted living facility where they have dance classes and happy hour.

Mama then ends up these visits by announcing that

she is happy that Daddy is dead because now, she can start to live. With that pronouncement, Mama gets up from the living room and goes into the kitchen, and starts doing the dishes. At that point, the condolence visits are over.

Needless to say, word of what Mama said at these visits quickly got back to me, my sister, and my brother. They are now very angry with Mama because of what she said about Daddy to all these people. I understand how they feel but I think that we need to understand that Mama is old and not in her right mind, so we need to ignore what she says.

Also, my brother and sister do not want to sell the family home which is on the water with about five acres and is worth a lot of money. They want to keep the family home with Mama in it until Mama dies. Then, they want to sell it all, make a lot of money which will go in equal shares to us children. They definitely do not want Mama to sell the house now and go into this very nice assisted living facility because it costs a lot of money, and they are afraid that there will be nothing left from the sale of the house for them by the time that Mama dies.

Mama has told us all that she is not yet cold in her grave and that she is going to sell the house and move and that we can all be pleased or displeased about it. I am the oldest and have always been the one child who helped Daddy and Mama with everything, so it will fall on me to decide what to do and make all the arrangements.

I want Mama to be happy and safe, but I don't want to make my brother and sister angry with me. What should we do about Mama?

ANSWER:  This house belongs to your mother, and she should be able to do with it as she chooses.  At 92 years of age, your mother would be safer and better cared for in a good assisted living facility rather than living alone in her own home.

If your mother wants to sell her home and move into an assisted living facility now, help her do it.  Your brother and sister, who sound more than a little greedy, won't like it, but so what.  It is more important that your mother be happy and safe now than your brother and sister have lots of money sometime down the road after your mother dies.

So, go help your Mama pack up, sell the house, and move into the nice assisted living facility.  It will be a tremendous amount of work for you, but as my mother used to say, you will be earning jewels in your crown in heaven because it is the right thing to do.

# WALKING INTO THE FIRE

**June 14**

Two years ago, I met the man of my dreams – rich, good-looking, older, and sophisticated.  It was love at first sight, and we were seriously involved with each other ever since our first date.  We talked about getting married, and each of us wanted to have three or four children, and he also said that he wanted me to be a stay-at-home mother and wife.

On Valentine's Day, he proposed to me, and I was so very happy to accept him.  We set the wedding date for June 16, and I had made all the arrangements for the wedding when last week, disaster struck.

Last Tuesday, my fiancé came over to my house for dinner and to talk about some final details of the wedding.  After dinner, he seemed very nervous, and then, he took out a Prenuptial Agreement from his brief case and told me that he wanted me to sign this agreement before we got married.  It was a lot of legal mumbo jumbo, and I could not understand all of it, so I told him that I would have to bring it to an attorney so he or she could explain it to me.

My fiancé got mad and told me that there wasn't time for all that because the wedding date was just around the corner. He also said that I would need to sign this Prenuptial Agreement very soon because he would not marry me without it being signed. Then, he stomped out of my house.

Now, my fiancé is a wealthy man with numerous investments and businesses while I am 20 years younger and have a whole lot less money than him. He also has a lot more education than I do and understands business and legal stuff a lot better than I do.

Although I was just going to go ahead and sign the Prenuptial Agreement, my mother insisted that I take it to her attorney for him to look at it. My mother and I set up a meeting with this attorney, and he said that if I signed this Prenuptial Agreement, I would give up my right to post-separation support, alimony, and equitable distribution if the marriage didn't work out as well as my right to claim anything from my husband's estate if my husband died before me and we were still married. The Prenuptial Agreement also said that everything my fiancé owned now or would earn later on during the marriage was his separate property and that I would get none of it in the event of a separation or if he died before me.

The attorney said that if I signed this Prenuptial Agreement, I would be undertaking all of the responsibilities of marriage without getting any of the financial benefits of being married. He also said that I should not sign this Prenuptial Agreement unless I wanted to work all my life for this man and get nothing except a bunch of kids in return.

The marriage is approaching, and my fiancé is really yelling at me to sign this Prenuptial Agreement. I love my fiancé and want to marry him, but I am not sure what I should do about this Prenuptial Agreement. What do you recommend?

ANSWER:  The question that you need to ask yourself is why would you want to marry someone who is setting you up for financial disaster at the very start of your marriage?  People usually wait until they separate to start trying to rip each other off but, he is doing just that to you even before you take that long walk together down the aisle.

Another thing to look at is how does your fiancé love, honor, and cherish you in that Prenuptial Agreement? How does he plan to care for you in sickness and in health?  How does he plan to support you when you have three or four children and he dies or takes off with someone who is thirty years younger and has fewer wrinkles and stretch marks than you?

Obviously, he doesn't want to provide for you in any way once you are married to him or after you are separated from him.  He wants you to assume all the financial risks of this marriage while he assumes all the financial benefits.

If you sign this Prenuptial Agreement, you will be bound by its terms, and you will have no financial security as the wife of this man.  Is that the kind of marriage you want?

I would strongly recommend against signing this Prenuptial Agreement even if it means that your fiancé calls the whole thing off.  His refusal to marry you could be the biggest blessing in disguise that you ever had in your life.

You need to ask yourself this question:  When a man truly loves a woman, is this the kind of agreement that two weeks before the wedding, he tries to get her to sign?

# NO GOOD DEED GOES UNPUNISHED

**June 21**

I am not trying to be greedy. I am just trying to get my rights and what is fair.

When my husband's parents got old and feeble, we all agreed that I would quit my job cleaning condos on the beach and tend to them during the day at their house. His parents said that they could not afford to pay me to care for them, but when they died, they would give their house to my husband and I as sort of a back payment for the care that I would give them. Since we all agreed, we did not sign any papers about it.

So for five years, I cooked their meals, cleaned their house, gave them their medicine, drove them to their doctors, and helped them get dressed, take baths, and get places that they wanted to go. As they both got sicker, the work got harder with changing diapers and dressings and all of that mess.

Finally, my father-in-law died earlier this year, and my mother-in-law followed him less than a month later. At the time, I thought it was a blessing because all of that work was killing me.

As it turned out, my husband's parents did not have wills, and my husband is their only child. So, he was the one appointed by the court to pay their bills and settle their estate.

Last month, their house was finally sold. After all the bills were paid, there was about $100,000.00 left for me and my husband. I told my husband that I wanted to use my one-half of the money to buy a good used car to replace my old bomber which had started to make horrible, expensive-sounding noises and had terrible gas mileage. I also wanted to pay off my credit card bills and put the rest into savings.

When I asked my husband for my one-half share, he got really angry with me and said that all of the $100,000.00 was his because it was his inheritance from his parents and that he was not going to give me any of it. Instead, he was going to replace his two year old truck with a brand new truck and buy another brand new boat. He said that he didn't think that there would be any money left over after he got his new truck and boat, and that even if there was, he would not give me any of it because it was all his money.

He also said that he did not remember any agreement about my getting one-half of the money from his parents' house in exchange for my caring for them. He said that I didn't want to work full-time cleaning houses and that I quit my job so that I could stay home full-time and that I didn't do that much for his parents during the last five years.

I could not believe that he was saying these things when I had sweated and slaved for his parents for five years while he did almost nothing for them. I argued, yelled, and pleaded with him to give me my one-half share, and he absolutely will not give me any of it. He says that he has talked with an attorney who said that this inheritance was his alone and his separate property and that I, as his wife, am not entitled to any of it.

Can this be true? Do I as his wife have any rights to one-half of this money?


ANSWER:  Unfortunately for you, North Carolina law is quite clear that your husband's inheritance from his parents is his separate property, and you, as his wife, do not have a right to any of it.  So, your husband is entitled to keep all of his inheritance and does not have to give you one single cent of it because you are his spouse.

However, you may be able to get some money out of your husband but you would have to file a law suit against your husband for breach of contract, unjust enrichment, and other equitable remedies.  Suing your own husband is expensive and stressful, and you may not win your law suit against him since there is no written agreement and his parents are dead and cannot testify on your behalf.

So, you have really been taken advantage of by your husband, and unless you sue him and win, there is nothing that you can do to collect your one-half share of this money.

The unfortunate truth is that you should have had this agreement written up and signed by everyone so that your one-half interest in your in-laws' house was protected.  You did not do so, and your husband has taken full advantage of your willingness to help his parents and your failure to get this agreement in writing.

Next time, if there is one, get any agreement involving financial matters with your husband in writing and get an attorney to write it.

This has been a hard and expensive lesson. As the old saying goes, "We get too soon old and too late smart."

# WHEN MORAL AND LEGAL OBLIGATIONS DIFFER

**June 28**

When our son was born, my wife and I were pretty crushed to the ground when we found out that he had Down's Syndrome.  Over time, I think that I adjusted better to the situation than my wife, and I became my son's main caretaker.  My son now goes to a special high school for children with disabilities, and he works hard to learn the things that he is able to learn.  However, he is profoundly disabled and will never be able to financially support himself.

Two years ago, my wife started weight training at a gym and began running several miles a day because she said that she wanted to get in shape.  What I later learned was that she was doing more running around with buff young jocks than anything else and that she was losing weight so that she could bait her hook more effectively.

It was when she started traveling all over the state on weekends for "competitions" that I started to wonder just exactly what was going on.  Almost every weekend, my wife left to run at these 5k or 10k road races while I stayed home with our son.  I now ask myself what was wrong with that picture.

So, when my wife announced earlier this year that she had fallen in love with one of her "iron men" and was leaving me and my son, it did not come as such a big surprise.

What did surprise me was the fact that my wife does not want to pay me child support since our son will turn 18 next month. She said that she didn't have to pay anything for his support when he is over 18 years of age and legally an adult.

My wife told me that she had a lot of additional expenses with her new apartment and that she was going to enter some national triathlons which are very expensive, so she had no money to give me for our son's expenses.

Hell flew in me when I heard that garbage. I told her that this was her son that she was talking about and that she had a legal obligation to support him all of his life because he was disabled and would never be able to work and support himself. I told her that she would help pay for our son or I would see her in court. In response, she walked out of our house and slammed the door hard.

What I need to know is how I can make her pay child support to me for our son. I don't make that much money because I am his caretaker, and things will be very tight financially if his mother doesn't pay child support for his care. Isn't our disabled son entitled to child support from his mother?

ANSWER: In North Carolina, a parent is only required to support his or her child until that child turns 18 unless the child is still in primary or secondary school at age 18. Then, the parent has to continue to pay child support until the child graduates, stops attending school on a regular basis, fails to make satisfactory progress towards graduation, or reaches age 20, whichever comes first.  After the child turns 18, the court can also order that these child support payments stop at any time for good cause.

So, your wife is obligated to pay child support to you for your son until your son turns 20 so long as he is in a school program and making progress of some sort. Your son does not have to be in a regular school program but can be in a special school or program for disabled children in order for your wife to have an obligation to support your son until he turns 20.

After your son turns 20, your wife has no obligation to support him. Unfortunately, you will have to bear the financial burdens for your son after he turns 20 if your wife does not want meet her moral obligation to support her disabled son.

In order to get the child support ball rolling, you should immediately contact the Carteret County Child Support Office, and these highly effective folks will act on your behalf to get a court order for child support from your wife.  You should also check with the local social security office to see what financial help might be available for your son when he becomes an adult.

As an additional source of funds, you should also see a family law attorney to see if you are a dependent spouse and eligible for post-separation support and alimony from your wife.  Further, you should ask this attorney if you should ask for an unequal distribution of your marital assets in your favor.

Finally, don't waste your time arguing with your wife

about her obligation to support your son. Selfishly, she has chosen to leave you and your son and go pump another man's iron, and she only wants what is fun and convenient for her. You need to focus your energy on yourself and your son and let the Carteret County Child Support office and your family law attorney jerk a knot in your wife and make her pay to support her son in a variety of ways.

# MOVE FROM KNOWLEDGE AND STRENGTH

## July 5

When my husband told me last month that he was leaving me and the kids, I couldn't believe it. We had been married for 10 years, had three great children, owned a lovely home and 2 nice cars, and had money in the bank. As a couple, I thought that we were doing fine.

I was wrong.

A week after he told me that he was not happy and was leaving, he was gone. Devastated doesn't begin to describe how the kids and I feel.

Also, my husband is the bread winner in the family, and I have never worked outside the house since our first child was born 8 years ago. The few job skills that I have would never get me a living wage in today's job market. I am terrified that I will end up working minimum wage jobs, living in a cheap rental house, and buying everything I need at thrift stores for the rest of my life.

I also still love my husband and want him back not only for me but for our three kids. I don't want our children to be raised in a broken home and suffer all the many things that kids from divorced families have to endure.

Last week, my husband gave me a Separation Agreement and Property Settlement that his attorney drafted, and I don't begin to understand most of the legal gobbley-gook in it. I asked my husband to please not start the legal stuff right away but instead, I wanted for us to go to a marriage counselor and try to get our marriage back on track.

In response, he told me that he still loved me and was willing to go to a marriage counselor and try to work on our marriage provided that I sign this Separation Agreement now so that some things are worked out before we get back together. He also told me that I really didn't need take on the great expense of having an attorney look at this Separation Agreement for me because he (my husband) had taken care of everything fairly in this Separation Agreement. My husband then said that I should trust him to do the right thing for me.

When I told him that I would have to think about whether or not I was going to sign the Separation Agreement, my husband got really mad. He started yelling that my acting in this stubborn and selfish way was one of the reasons why he had left me. He then said that if I was good to him, trusted him, and signed this Separation Agreement, he would want to try and reconcile with me, but not before I signed this Separation Agreement.

I feel that I am in a no-win situation. I still love my husband and want to reconcile with him, but I don't want to sign the Separation Agreement when I don't know my rights and don't understand most of the terms in this Separation Agreement. I want to trust my husband, and yet, I am afraid that he is not being honest about the terms in the Separation Agreement being fair to me. What should I do?

### ANSWER:  DO NOT SIGN THIS SEPARATION AGREEMENT!

You need to immediately meet with a family law attorney and have him or her review the Separation Agreement to make sure that you and your children are protected by its terms.  Do not sign this Separation Agreement or any other legal document that your husband might give you to sign without your attorney looking at it first and giving you an opinion as to what it means and how the terms will affect you and the children.

You are right to not trust your husband.  He has left you and the children, and you can bet the rent, that he is not looking out for your financial interests and well-being.   Instead, your husband is all about looking out for Number One.

Also, don't be fooled with your husband saying that he wants to try and reconcile with you because he is probably only using this line in order to get you to sign this Separation Agreement.  When a spouse wants to reconcile, he or she usually talks about going to a marriage counselor first and not about signing a Separation Agreement as a condition to marriage counseling.

Your husband is just singing his current sweet song because he wants you to sign this Separation Agreement which, as the old country western song goes, very likely gives him the gold mine and gives you the shaft.

Don't fall for his manipulative approach.  Be strong and just say no to your husband's browbeating.  See an attorney and learn what your rights are in your present situation and what you should do next.  Move from knowledge and strength, not from ignorance and weakness.

# THE STINKING RAT'S REVENGE

**July 12**

If my husband had been meat, he'd of been road kill. He was so mean and stinky, and of course, he only thought of tending to Number One, namely himself.

But I stuck with him, mostly for his money and the house we lived in. Finally, after forty very long years, he died. I was so happy that it was very hard to keep a sad face when people told me how sorry they were that he had died. Not me! I was glad! The only thing that I was sorry about is that he didn't die thirty years ago.

So, I was looking forward to having all his money plus a big chunk of cash from his life insurance policy. We had paid on that life insurance policy for years and years, and it had a $100,000.00 pay out when he died. My husband had always promised me that he had put me as the beneficiary of this life insurance policy and that this money would all be mine when he bit the dust.

After he finally went to his just reward, I got a nasty shock when I learned that my husband had changed the beneficiary of this life insurance policy from me to a woman who I knew nothing about and who appeared to have been his lover for at least 10 years. I don't care that she got it on with my husband because I was just grateful that she ran interference for me from my husband's gropings and snortings.

However, I really did care that she was named as the beneficiary of that $100,000.00 life insurance policy because that money is supposed to be mine. I want that money, and I put up with a lot of you-know-what in order to get it. I outlived that sorry rat! How can I get that money from his girl friend who doesn't deserve it?


ANSWER: If the girl friend put up with The Stinking Rat's gropings and snortings for 10 years, she may well have rightly earned this $100,000.00.

As it is, The Stinking Rat has named her, and not you, as the beneficiary on this life insurance policy. Consequently, the life insurance company must pay the $100,000.00 from this policy to her and not to you. You have no claim on it, and there is nothing you can do to change this situation.

Perhaps if you had been more amenable to The Stinking Rat's gropings and snortings, there would have been no girl friend, and you would have had all of the $100,000.00 for yourself.

However, what's done is done, and you will have to content yourself with getting the rest of The Stinking Rat's estate, and give up any thought of getting that $100,000.00 into your hands.

Unfortunately, your marriage shows the truth of the Bible verse, "Where your treasure is, there will your heart be also."

# CATCHING FLIES WITH HONEY

### July 19

When my son's wife left him, we were not surprised. She was always drinking and running with a fast crowd when my son was in the military and stationed overseas. When my son decided to marry her in spite of her hooting around, my wife and I were not happy since we felt that there wasn't much to her and that she came from even less.

But my son and she got married, and they had this wonderful little boy who has been the light of our lives. Their marriage stayed rocky, and finally ended when she took off with our grandson to live with another man.

Of course, there was a big court fight over custody of our then three year old grandson. Since our son was still in the military and was going to be deployed again overseas, his wife got custody of the child, and our son got visitation which was described in great detail in a court order.

Since we wanted to be on good terms with our son's estranged wife, we tried to stay out of it all, but the more time went by, the less we liked our daughter-in-law, and I guess she knew it. Soon, she wouldn't let us talk to our grandson on the phone when we called or see him when we asked to pick him up, so we just talked and saw him when our son had visitation with the child.

We knew that we could go to court to get some kind of grandparents' rights, but we decided to not cause or look for trouble with her because the custody trial was over and we just wanted to stay out of court for our grandson's sake.

Then two years after the court order was entered, our son was killed in a car accident, and we were devastated. His wife allowed our grandson to come to our son's funeral, but since then, she has refused our requests to see our grandson.

It has now been six months since our son died, and his wife still says that we have no right to see our five year old grandson and that she is tired of dealing with us and that we had better stop calling her about our grandson because she will charge us with harassing phone calls if we keep it up. I can't believe that anyone could be so cruel and hateful but she is.

We don't want custody of our grandson and we don't want to take our grandson away from his mother. We just want to spend a day or so with him every month and be able to call him and see him some during holidays.

What can we do now to get our grandparents' rights for visitation so we can see our grandson?

ANSWER: Unfortunately, you are no longer entitled to court-ordered grandparents' visitation because custody of your grandson had been resolved through a court order, and at the time of your son's death, custody was not in dispute between him and his wife.

Additionally, you and your wife did not pursue your grandparents' rights for visitation with your grandson when his custody was being litigated by your son and daughter-in-law. As a result, neither your wife or you are parties in this custody law suit, and the court order does not mention you or your visitation rights at all.

If you had filed suit for grandparents' visitation or if the custody order had outlined some visitation rights for you, you would now have the right to go back in and ask the court to enforce your grandparents' visitation or to modify the visitation order if you could show that there had been a substantial change of circumstances adversely or positively affecting the child since the last visitation order was entered. However, you did not pursue your grandparents' rights, so your daughter-in-law is now within her legal rights to not allow you to see your grandson.

This law is very harsh and makes the loss of your son even harder to bear because now, you have in effect lost your grandson as well as your son.

One way to try and get back into your grandson's life is to basically buy your way in. You could call your daughter-in-law and offer to pay for your grandson's day care costs, or school clothes, or whatever it is that your grandson needs that your daughter-in-law is willing to let you provide.

If you pay a bunch of money on your grandson's behalf and are very sweet about it, your daughter-in-law may agree to let you spend some time with your grandson. Just be sure to grit your teeth and be very nice to your daughter-in-law the entire time and never make any rude or snide remarks about her to your grandson or within the hearing of your grandson since that kind of thing tends to come back and haunt the speaker.

It also wouldn't hurt if you bought your daughter-in-law some pretty nice presents at Christmas, Mother's Day, and on her birthday. Be good to her and bribe her, and hopefully, she will be good to you and let you see your grandson.

If she still won't let you see your grandson, the only other way to see him is to try and get custody of him through the court. Then, you will have a huge, expensive, and destructive legal battle with your daughter-in-law because you will have to file a new law suit and allege and prove that your daughter-in-law is an unfit parent and/or that she has acted in a manner inconsistent with her protected status as a parent. You will need to get a good family law attorney to see if that is a road that you want to go down.

So, try the easy non-legal way first, and make it clear to your daughter-in-law that many financial benefits will be hers and your grandson's if you and your wife can be a part of your grandson's life. Be sweet to your daughter-in-law and do not argue with her because she has the power to keep your grandson away from you both until he turns 18.

Just remember that your daughter-in-law will probably be a fly that you need to catch with honey and not vinegar.

# WHEN YOU PLAY, YOU PAY

**July 26**

I have been married for thirty years to the same person, and while she is an OK person and has never cheated on me, she is boring, especially in bed. She's had four kids and looks it, and she won't get into the swinging scene even though I was really interested in trying it out. Instead, she just is a stay-at-home wife who cleans, cooks, and wears frumpy clothes and arch supports.

So, I started surfing the net for a little extra on the side, if you know what I mean. I got lots of nibbles on my hook and I was having my cake and eating it too without my wife knowing anything. It was great!

Since my wife was completely ignorant about computers or the internet and I was away on business a lot, I thought the coast was clear for me to have a little time off for bad behavior. Over the 4th of July, I was away on business and shot off my roman candle quite a bit and saw plenty of fireworks.

When I got home, I finally corralled my wife into bed because I knew that I was man enough for all the ladies in my life. I tried to get my wife to try some of the things that I had recently learned but she just looked at me like I had lost my mind.  We had a big fight, and I just decided that enough was enough and walked out the door.

I found an apartment and have been having a great time being single until two days ago when I got served with a law suit from my wife.  My wife apparently wants lots of permanent alimony and most of the assets that we have accumulated during the marriage.  She also stated that I had committed adultery numerous times and described all of my internet activity in some explicit detail.

It was actually embarrassing because my behavior sounded a lot worse in print than what it actually was. I was also surprised that my wife had hired a computer expert to check out my computer and download and print a lot of things that I never thought would see the light of day including some photographs of me that are pretty graphic and highly compromising.

Now, I am getting worried because I don't want to pay my wife anything in  alimony, never mind permanent alimony.  I have worked all my life while she just stayed at home raising our four kids and keeping the house.  She has never worked.  However, I figure that she can go out and get a job someplace, particularly if she would lose about thirty pounds.  Why should I support someone who chose to stay home and live off the fat of the land, namely me?

How can I avoid paying her alimony?


ANSWER:   Since you have been the supporting spouse and your wife has been the dependent spouse throughout your marriage, you are about to learn that if you play, you pay.

Additionally, you have committed adultery while your wife has been faithful during the marriage, and your wife did not forgive or condone your adultery, so in North Carolina, you are very likely on the hook for alimony to your wife. Further, it sounds as if your wife has all the evidence she needs and then some to back up her claims of adultery against you.

You need to suck it up and pay your wife alimony. She blessed you with four children and thirty long years of her life. She stayed at home and provided you and your children with a comfortable home life, and as a result, she did not accumulate any retirement, financial accounts, or social security of her own.

You need to avoid a trial in court. Just imagine sitting in the witness chair and having to identify to the judge who are the people in these photographs and what it is that you are doing with them. You would not just be hooked with alimony, you would be gaffed.

Get an attorney and settle this case including your wife's claim for alimony. You are now paying for sowing your wild oats, and you may not think that they were worth it once all is said and done. Just remember, as you sow, so shall you reap.

# CATCHING THE BIG ONE

**August 2**

It all began this spring when I caught one of the biggest marlins in a fishing tournament. That night, I celebrated in a big way in a bar in Beaufort and met this young lady who was impressed with my large fish and wanted to party. The beer flowed like the incoming tide until early in the morning, and then, this girl decided that she wanted to charm my wild snake, so she did.

After that lost weekend, we continued to see each other and charm the snake until in June, she told me that she was pregnant with my child. Strangely enough, I was really excited about the baby. I am 28 and have never been married and do not have any children, so when she told me that she was carrying my child, I was even happier than when I caught that big marlin.

I went out shopping with my girl friend and bought all kinds of maternity clothes for her and paid for her entire obstetrician's bill which was not cheap. I started looking at baby stuff like cribs, car seats, and changing tables because I wanted to buy them well before the baby was born. I was really psyched to be a dad.

But then, this girl told me that she was not going to

keep the baby because she was only 21 years old and did not want the responsibility for caring for this child. I told her that I would take the child and raise him or her but she said I would never see or raise this child because she had contacted an adoption agency and was planning to give this child up for adoption right after he or she was born.

I begged her to not do that and asked her to let me have the child and she could see the child whenever she wanted to and she would not have to pay me child support. She said that she wouldn't agree to those terms because she was giving this child up for adoption and that was that.

After this discussion, we broke up and our relationship was over but I have continued to give her money for her vitamins and maternity clothes. I also got a two bedroom apartment so that I could keep the baby after he or she is born and have started to furnish the baby's bedroom. My parents are really excited about the baby who will be their first grandchild, and my Mom is helping me paint the baby's room and pick out baby furniture.

The problem is how can I make sure that I get to see and keep the baby after it is born because my former girl friend is still saying that she is going to give this baby up for adoption and there is nothing that I can do about it.

Is that true? Is there anything that I can do to make sure that I have a say about the adoption? What do I have to do to get custody of my child?

ANSWER: If you want custody of your child, you need to act now and be sure to do all the right things in order to protect your rights to your child and to keep the Snakecharmer from giving away your baby.

In North Carolina, the adoption agency will have to file a petition in court to terminate your parental rights and get your rights terminated by a judge before the adoption can be completed. In order to help preserve your rights to this child, you need to do at least one of the following:

> 1.  Provide substantial financial support or consistent care to the mother and child during her pregnancy and after the child is born.
>
> 2.  File a Petition to legitimate this child with the Carteret County Clerk of Court as soon as the child is born.
>
> 3.  File a law suit to establish paternity and custody of the minor child.
>
> 4.  Marry the mother of the child.

So far, you have done the right thing by providing substantial support to the Snakecharmer by paying for her maternity clothes, vitamins, and obstetric bill and by giving her money. You have also spent money by getting a place for the baby to live and by buying furnishings for the baby's room. You need to keep this up and continue to give money to the Snakecharmer and finish decorating the baby's room and keep buying things for the baby.

Be sure to give the Snakecharmer a check or money order (no cash!) so that you can document that you have given her money. You also need to save your receipts for everything that you buy for the Snakecharmer, the baby's room and for the baby.

Additionally, you need to get a lawyer and have him or her ready to file the petition to legitimate and the lawsuit to determine paternity and custody as soon as possible after the baby is born. Don't delay even a day after the baby is born. The adoption agency will be waiting in the wings to file their petition to terminate your parental rights as soon as the baby is born, so don't let them beat you to the Courthouse.

Once the baby is born, your parents could also ask the court in your custody law suit to award them visitation with the child because of their rights as grandparents. In this way, they could try to preserve their rights to see this child.

Additionally, you now need to change your lifestyle a bit so that you rein in the wild snake, drink less, and stop seeking out itinerant snakecharmers, Fish more, frolic less.

Keep doing the right things for your child because your child needs you and your family. You will only have one chance to do this whole thing right, and if you don't, your parental rights will very likely be terminated and you will never see this child again. The stakes are high. Fight the good fight and get custody of your child.

# WALKING THE RIGHTEOUS PATH

**August 9**

When my son told me that smoking marijuana every day made him a better parent of his five month old son, I couldn't believe it. He said that it made him calmer and more relaxed. I told him that his drug use was making him more irresponsible and unable to care for his child.

I have known for some time that my son and his girl friend were doing drugs and drinking to excess. So when they had a baby this year, I was really worried that they would not be able to smoke dope every day, booze it up regularly, and successfully care for their child.

Unfortunately, I was right.

Since the child was born, they have not properly cared for the baby. They frequently drop him off at my house so they can go and party. Often, they don't come and get him for several days. I never know when they are coming back, and when I ask them, they just say "Later".

And the poor child – he is so scrawny and doesn't seem happy. When the drop him off with me, he frequently has a bad diaper rash and is so hungry. A lot of the time, he is dirty and so are his clothes.

The last straw was last week when I got a call from a complete stranger who said that she had been keeping my grandson for the last four days because my son and his girl friend had never come back for the baby like they had said they would. This woman was calling me to try and find these sorry parents to tell them to come and pick up their child.

So, I went to this woman's trailer and got my grandson. He was a mess – dirty, a bad diaper rash, and really tired. This woman said that the baby had been very fussy and had seemed to have a cough, so she had been giving him cough syrup (adult strength) to help him sleep.

I took my grandson home and thought, enough is enough. I cannot give my grandson back to my son and his girl friend. They are terrible parents and do not seem to care for this child.

What can I do to keep my grandson and protect him from his parents?

ANSWER: You need to run, not walk, to a good family law attorney and file suit asking for custody of your grandson. You also need to get emergency temporary custody of the child right away so that his parents cannot take him away from you.

You will have to show the court that the parents are unfit due to their regular drug and alcohol abuse and due to the numerous ways in which they failed to properly feed, clothe, and care for their baby.

You should also be able to show the court that the parents acted in manner inconsistent with their protected status as a parent. In other words, they didn't act like parents but instead dumped their child on other people to care for him.

In your law suit, you should also ask the court to order that the parents only have supervised visitation with the child, and that the parents be required to have random full panel drug tests and substance abuse evaluations and that the results of these tests and evaluations be given to you.

You also need to take the child immediately to a pediatrician so that the doctor can check the child for possible physical injuries and to make sure that his immunizations are up to date.

You are doing the right thing. In taking this child into your custody, you are very likely saving this child's life both physically and emotionally.

Raising your grandson will be a tremendous amount of work, but he needs you desperately and is undoubtedly worth the effort. Further, you are, as my mother still says, earning jewels in your crown in heaven by taking the hard but righteous path in caring for and raising up your grandson.

# WHAT GOES AROUND COMES AROUND

**August 16**

When my boyfriend left his wife for me last year, it was the best move that he ever made. However, his wife told him that she was going to make him pay, and she has tried every which way to do just that.

After he moved out and moved in with me, his wife immediately went to Carteret County Child Support Enforcement, and she got a court order requiring him to pay a boat load of money to her for his four kids. I told him that the amount of money was highway robbery and that he should fight it, but he said that there was nothing that he could do about it. Now every two weeks, they take out so much money from my boyfriend's paycheck to pay his child support to his wife that he can hardly pay for his truck and boat payments. It is very unfair!

So now, his wife has finally got off her fat butt and found a job. That is the good news, but the bad news is that she has taken my boyfriend back to court for an increase in child support because she says that she now has day care expenses for the kids since she has started working full-time. The amount that she pays for day care is ridiculously high, and my boyfriend did not have any say in where the kids were put in day care.

For a whole lot less money, my 14 year old niece could have taken care of these kids at my sister's trailer after school and during the summer while my niece watches her three younger brothers, but my boyfriend's wife wouldn't even consider it. This woman is so unreasonable!

My boyfriend's wife just refuses to get over the fact that she was not woman enough for her husband and I am. She won't recognize the fact that my boyfriend is finally happy and moving on with his life with me. Instead, she is trying to do everything she can to break him financially and make him miserable. I have told my boyfriend that he has got to stop her from being so greedy.

What does my boyfriend have to do in order to prevent his wife from getting an increase in child support from him?

ANSWER: To avoid paying an increase in child support, your boyfriend could come to his senses, fall on his knees before his wife, beg her forgiveness, implore her to take him back again, and move back in with his wife and children. However, you will undoubtedly ensure that little scenario never occurs.

So instead, her husband will have to pay an increase in child support if his wife can show that there has been a change in circumstances due to the increased needs of the children since the last order was entered.

In other words, his wife will have to show that she is now regularly paying certain amounts for child care for the children while she is at work and that she was not paying these monies when she last went to court and got a court order for child support.

If she can prove that she is now paying for work-related child care for their children, she can get an increase in child support and there is nothing that her husband or you can do about it.

Further, there is every reason why her husband should help pay for day care when he was the one who left his wife and four children and created the situation where she had to go back to work outside the home and pay for day care.

If her husband can't pay for his truck and boat payments because of his child support obligation, that is just too bad. Why should his truck and boat payments come before the needs of his children?

Finally, it would only be your just reward if you, having been woman enough to lure him away from his wife and family, ended up as the woman who had to help your boyfriend pay for his obligations to his family.

# AVOIDING THE FIERY PATH
# OF SELF-DESTRUCTION

**August 23**

When I married my husband three years ago, I knew that he smoked marijuana from time to time, but I thought that he would stop this bad habit out of love for me because he knew that I didn't like it.

I was wrong. Not only did my husband not stop smoking dope, but instead, he started smoking dope every day and began using cocaine and crack several times a week.

My husband also started hanging out with a really bad bunch of people who drank too much, used a lot of illegal drugs, and took every kind of prescription pill that they could get their hands on.

My husband went from a good-looking man to a scrawny, twitchy bastard with a hair trigger temper. He never seemed to have enough money and was always bugging me to give him $30.00 or $40.00. I started hiding my purse when I was at home because he would help himself to all the money in my wallet whenever he could get his hands on it.

Last month, I found out that he had taken out money from our equity line on our house to the tune of

$12,000.00 and had racked up our joint credit card to over $8,000.00 with cash advances. I did not know anything about these cash advances because my husband had been hiding the monthly statements from me for the last two months.

When I confronted my husband about these debts, he refused to tell me what he had used the money for. Instead, he got in my face and yelled at me that it was none of my business and to shut up before he shut me up.

More and more, he stays out late and sometimes doesn't come home at all until the next day. Most of the time, he looks terrible with dark circles under his eyes and shaking hands.

The last straw came two weeks ago when he began selling drugs out of our home. A lot of horrible people started coming by the house and meeting with my husband. They only stay a few minutes with my husband in our spare bedroom, and then, they leave. My husband has put a double bolt lock on the this bedroom door and has told me not to go into this room at all. When I ask him what he is doing in there, he just tells me that he is "working" and to shut up.

I feel like the person that I married is gone, and in his place, a devil has appeared. I am afraid all the time, and am just grateful that we do not have any children together. What do I need to do to leave my husband and get out of this terrible marriage?

ANSWER: You are in a dangerous situation and need to act quickly.

By selling drugs from your home, your husband has endangered you since some of his customers might not mind hurting or killing people in your house if they could get your husband's supply of drugs and cache of money.

Since your husband very likely will not move out of your house, you need to leave first in order to protect yourself. Wait until he is gone for several hours, and then have a mover come and take everything that belonged to you before the marriage and one-half of the things that you both purchased during the marriage with marital funds.

You will only get one chance to do this move and get your stuff, so do it right and don't forget anything. Then, do not tell him where you have moved. If this is a good time to move out of state, do it. The further away that you can get from this man, the better and safer you will be.

As soon as you have moved, call your equity line lender and freeze the equity line so that your husband cannot get any more money out of this account. Then, call your joint credit card company and cancel the account so that your husband can no longer charge anything or get cash advances.

Cancel every joint financial account so that your husband can no longer charge anything that is in your name. If there are joint savings accounts or other financial assets in both of your names, take all of the money out of these joint accounts and put the money in an account in your name alone. Do not spend this money, but keep it safe so that it will be available during equitable distribution.

You will also need to get a lawyer to advise you, so it would be a good idea to meet with a good family law attorney before you leave to ensure that you have protected yourself as much as possible.

Once you have moved, you should file suit for a division of the marital assets and debts. Your husband will probably need a kick in the butt in order to get him to divide these assets and debts with you, and your lawyer should certainly be able to do just that.

After your move, keep an eye out for your estranged husband. If he is following you while you are driving, call 911. Keep a camera with you all the times in your purse so you can photograph him if he is following you. If he comes to your door and knocks, do not let him in but instead, move away from the door into another room and call 911. You need to be very careful of him because you are now a witness to his drug use and drug trafficking. He and the people whom he works for will probably be very interested in having you keep your mouth shut about his drug trafficking, and they may not have many scruples as to how your silence is achieved.

Your husband is walking on a fiery path of self-destruction. The flames are all around him, and there is nothing you can do to save him. You can, however, save yourself, and you should do so immediately. Get out of that house and get as much of your stuff as possible, but saving your stuff is not the priority. You can always get more stuff, but your safety and well-being should be your main concern. Run, don't walk to the nearest exit.

# THE LETTER OF THE LAW

## August 30

My thirty-five year old son was tricked into being a father by a heartless, conniving woman. On their very first date, she plied him with liquor and lured him into a situation where she had her way with him.

On top of it all, she falsely told him that she was using birth control, and then, she became pregnant!

After the baby boy was born, I had to pay almost $500.00 for genetic testing to see if my son was the father of this illegitimate child. Unfortunately, he was found to be 98.99% the father of this baby!

I told my son that it was not his fault that this predatory woman used him in such an infamous manner and that he should have nothing further to do with her or her illegitimate child. However, this woman has repeatedly called my son, who lives with me, and keeps asking him to send money to her for this child.

My son does not have much money because he has been overqualified for all of the jobs that he has had over the years. Also, the people who hire him rarely appreciate all of his fine qualities that are sometimes evident in his personality. They also usually fire him for no good reason.

So, my son does not have any money to give this grasping tramp who used her feminine wiles to lead my son into sin and who got herself into this situation. She got herself into this predicament, so let her get herself out of it!

However, a Sheriff's Department deputy came to my house at 6:30 yesterday morning, and served my poor son with a law suit from this overly fertile hussy who now is suing my son for child support. How can this be happening!

This greedy woman now wants my son to pay an incredible amount of child support to her every month until this baby is 18 years old. To put salt in the wounds, this fallen woman also wants my son to pay her attorney's fees for filing this law suit!

What an outrage! This shameless hussy lied and lured my naïve and unsuspecting son into fatherhood, and her behavior should not be rewarded with money every month for 18 years. She must be stopped!

How can I protect my son and prevent him from having to pay child support to this unprincipled wench who deserves a scarlet letter and nothing more?


ANSWER: In North Carolina, every child has the right to be supported by both of his or her parents. All the finger pointing and blame regarding who was responsible for the conception of the child is of no consequence because both parents must support that child.

Your son, who is a thirty-five year old man, voluntarily had unprotected sex with a woman, and as a result of his moment in the sun, fathered a son. He knew what he was doing with this woman, and he is responsible for the results of his sexual activity with her.

Your son must pay child support to the mother of his child or go to jail. It is that simple.

Your son must pay child support in the amount established by the North Carolina Child Support Guidelines. These guidelines use a formula which takes into account the parents' respective incomes, other children that either parent may be supporting, the child's work-related day care costs, the child's health insurance costs, and any extraordinary costs that the child might have.

The court will determine how much child support your son must pay, and then, your son must pay it or else face the consequences of wearing an orange jumpsuit and matching flip flops for a while.

So, your son should get a family law attorney to respond to this law suit and help him figure out an amount that he should pay in child support to the mother of his child. He needs to pay up and be a father to his son.

You need to take a pill or have a shot or something in order to have an attitude adjustment about your son and your grandson. Turn your son loose and let him be a man and a father instead of being immobilized in perpetual immaturity and irresponsibility by being tied to your apron strings.

You also need to think about your grandson and what kind of grandmother you are going to be to him. Do you want to care for, support, and nurture the next generation in your family, or do you want to harm, insult, and destroy it?

What kind of letter would you deserve if you continue to enable and smother your son and ignore your grandson?

# BE CAREFUL WHAT YOU ASK FOR

### September 6

Three years ago, I left my middle-aged wife and two teenage children for a much younger and more beautiful woman. At the time, it seemed like a great move to go from tough old rump roast to young, tender filet mignon.

However, I am beginning to think that I may have made a mistake since after my divorce from my old wife and my marriage to my young sweet thang, my new wife has been slowly but surely driving me into bankruptcy by her never-ending charges on my credit cards and by her refusal to work and make money. When I have asked her to economize a little more and get a job, she just laughs and tells me, "Sorry, baby. I am high maintenance. You are getting what you want from me, and I plan to do the same from you."

So, my new wife recently announced that I was about to become an even luckier man because she was planning to get heavy duty breast implants, liposuction, and fanny tucks so that she could be a real "Trophy Wife". Of course, my insurance won't pay for these $10,000.00 worth of "improvements" because they are voluntary. I tried to talk my wife out of these medical procedures because I can't afford them, but she just said that she would put them on one of my credit cards so my current lack of funds wouldn't be a problem.

I then told her that I would not agree to pay for these procedures or for her to use my credit cards to pay for them and that she could get a job, save her money, and pay for these "improvements" herself when she had the necessary funds. As soon as I told her that, my wife went ballistic and told me that I had to pay for her implants, liposuction, and fanny tuck because in North Carolina, a husband has to pay for all of his wife's medical bills.

She then looked at me and gave a little smile and said that I would be very happy and content if I didn't buck her and paid for her "improvements" but that I would be very sorry and have my credit ruined if I didn't pay for these bills. Then, she walked out of the room.

Can my new wife make me pay for her implants, liposuction, and fanny tuck, and do I, as her husband and a North Carolina resident, have to pay for any medical procedure that she wants?

ANSWER: In North Carolina, there is something called the Doctrine of Necessaries which applies equally to both husband and wife. This Doctrine states that each spouse, while married and living together, has an obligation to provide certain necessary items, including some medical services, for the other spouse.

However, there are limitations to this Doctrine since a spouse is only liable for the medical expenses that are "necessary". Grand Canyon cleavages, flat abs, and perky little butts are very likely not necessary under this Doctrine even if your spouse is a Trophy Wife. So, you are probably off the hook in terms of being legally obligated under this Doctrine to pay for your Trophy Wife's "improvements".

Nonetheless, you still have a problem. Your Trophy Wife is playing you like a fine old fiddle while she spends all your money and racks up your credit cards, but perhaps that is your just dessert for having chosen this type of person over your wife and children.

If you want to protect yourself financially and prevent your Trophy Wife from using all your money and maxing out your credit cards without your permission, you just need to close out your old financial accounts and credit cards and change these financial accounts and credit cards into your name alone. Then, Trophy Wife will not be able to spend and charge as she pleases with your money unless she gets your permission first.

You could also put Trophy Wife on a budget and give her a certain amount of money every month for her personal expenses. If you did these things, you probably know how long your Trophy Wife would remain lined up on your shelf, but that is another long story.

So, you are very likely not obligated in North Carolina under the Doctrine of Necessaries to pay for your Trophy Wife's breast implants, liposuction, and fanny tuck since these medical procedures are not "necessary". Perhaps you could give them to her as Christmas, birthday, and anniversary presents.

Finally, as a man who likes to compare his wives to meat, you might also consider what type of meat you most resemble. How about a Vienna sausage?

# WHEN VENUS BECOMES
# THE VENUS FLYTRAP

### September 13

The first time I saw my girlfriend, I knew she was the one.  She was surfing at the Cape, and when I saw her ride the cresting wave surrounded by foam, I thought that she was as beautiful as Venus rising out of the sea.

Of course I pursued her, but she played hard to get until finally, she succumbed due to my ardent wooing and two bottles of champagne.

So, we were soul mates and deeply in love.  Since neither of us were religious and were fairly anti-government, we decided not to get married and to not have our love legislated by the laws of North Carolina.  Instead, we lived together and had no intention of using marriage to legalize our love.

Five years ago, we decided to buy a house and got a very good deal on a great house on waterfront property.  We both put in equal amounts of money for a down payment and were both on the title of the property as tenants in common and on the mortgage as co-borrowers.

Time went by, and we were very happy until during last year, I began to notice that my girl friend was not that attentive to me and began to spend a lot of weekends away at her sister's house or so she said. She also encouraged me to visit my parents who live out of state while she stayed home.

It was when I found the photograph that I knew everything between my girl friend and I was over. In her bottom desk drawer under lots of papers, I found a photograph of my girl friend kissing another woman. When I confronted my girl friend, she freely admitted the relationship and told me that she had decided that she was bisexual and that I was just going to have to move out of our house so that her new female lover could move in with her.

It flew all over me when she said that, and I told her that I was not moving out of our house. She then said that I could stay but that I would have to move out of the master bedroom and go to one of the upstairs bedrooms so that her girl friend could move into the master bedroom with her. In that way, she said, we could all live together in the same house.

I told her that it would be a cold day in Hades before I would ever agree to that arrangement. I told her that we should sell the house, split the money that we made on the house, and go our separate ways.

She said that she would never agree to sell our house because she loved living next to the ocean and that we would just have to be mature about her relationship with her new one true love and live altogether in harmony. She told me that her love would be big enough to include both her girl friend and me.

I told her "Bull ****"!!

So, we are at a standstill.  I won't allow my girl friend's girl friend to move in and I won't leave, and my girl friend won't agree to sell our house.  My heart is broken, my life is a mess, and I am in a scrape!  Plus it is hard to sleep in the same bed with your girl friend when she only wants to do the wild thing with you in order to convince you to let her girl friend move in and live with you both.

What can I do to get this house sold, the mortgage paid off in full, one-half of the net proceeds from this house sale safely placed in my pocket, and my faithless girl friend out of my life?

ANSWER:  Since you never married The Venus Fly-trap, you are not entitled to ask the North Carolina court for equitable distribution which is the division between spouses of the parties' marital debts and assets.

Instead, you will have to petition the Clerk of Superior Court for a partition of the house and waterfront property which you own as tenants in common with The Venus Flytrap.  Your petition to partition needs to be filed in the county where your house is located and you should ask the court to order the sale of this property as soon as possible and to equally divide the net proceeds of the sale between you and The Venus Flytrap.

Needless to say, you should have an attorney represent you in this petition to partition and to also advise you on how to handle the situation you now face with The Venus Flytrap and her paramour.  Under no circumstance should you hit or threaten The Venus Flytrap since that bad behavior would give her the excuse she needs to have you removed from your house under the domestic violence statutes.

So, you should move into another bedroom, file your petition to partition, sit tight, behave yourself, and wait for the court to partition the property and order the sale of the house. Talk to and listen to your attorney's recommendations and follow them to the letter. This is not the time for self-help in removing various love interests from your home and pursuing legal actions on your own in court.

You might also consider seeing a counselor who could help you learn how to know if a woman is a real Venus or merely a Venus flytrap before you give your heart to her.

# WHAT NOT TO DO WHEN THE GRAVY TRAIN IS LEAVING THE STATION

## September 20

First of all, I want you to know that the problems in our marriage are not because I cannot get along with my husband. Oh no! I am a perfectly reasonable person and am able to get along with my husband just fine. The problems in our marriage are due to the fact that my husband simply cannot get along with me.

He argues with me all the time, yells and brandishes his whiskey glass when he does not get his way, and has been really unpleasant about the fact that I was fired from my last job (for no good reason!) two years ago and have not been able to find suitable employment since then. He also does not appreciate the fact that I do not like to cook or clean the house and that it is important to us that we go out to eat frequently at nice restaurants and have a housekeeper come in several times a week.

In short, my husband does not want to communicate with me – he just wants to bellow at me!

Last week, my husband told me that he wanted a divorce, handed me a Separation Agreement, and said that he wanted me to sign it right away. I think that he was angry about the fact that I frequently go out and use his credit cards to go to Raleigh and buy clothes that are suitable to our financial situation and status in our community. We live in a large and very expensive home in Pine Knoll Shores, and I need for my outfits to reflect the fact that my husband is a successful businessman. He knows better than to think that I am going to embarrass him and myself by being out in public in jeans and a T-shirt!

I also think that he was pretty incensed that I went to a local car dealership and bought myself a Cadillac using his name and credit without telling him. All I wanted to do was surprise him with my new car!

So now, all that my husband wants to do is yell at me and waive this Separation Agreement under my nose. He is also being very hateful by threatening to cancel his credit cards that I am using and to sell my beautiful new car. I am trying to be reasonable and get along with him, but it has not been easy.

I have been thinking that I should just go ahead and sign these papers to make my husband happy. I think that if I sign these papers, he will calm down and just forget about this whole divorce thing. What do you think? Should I sign these papers to keep peace in the family?

ANSWER: Earth to Wife! This is a Separation Agreement that he wants you to sign – not a love note!

Don't sign anything! Your husband wants to end his marriage to you, and your gravy train is about to leave the station. You need to contact an attorney right away and talk to him or her about what steps you should take in order to prepare yourself for a separation and a divorce.

It is a really unwise move to sign any legal document, especially one drafted by your irate husband's attorney, without having your attorney review it first. Your attorney could then let you know how much you stand to lose by signing this agreement which is almost certainly not going to protect your interests.

During the last few years, you have made some very poor financial decisions that have cost your husband a lot of money. Don't sign this agreement since its terms will surely contain your payback for having taken him so very effectively to the financial cleaners over the years.

As for your husband not being able to get along with you, you might ask yourself why he should be able to get along with someone who has taken full advantage of him every step of the way. Your husband probably wants a wife, not a user.

# HOW TO SQUEEZE
# MR. HOOTCHY-COOTCHY

**September 27**

For most of the seven years that I lived with my boyfriend, I was deceived. He told me that he loved me, that our relationship would last forever, and that he would help support me for the rest of my life.

We even bought a very expensive sports car together but titled it in his name because he said that his credit was better than mine, and that as a result, we could get a better interest rate using his name alone on the loan and car title. He said that the car would equally belong to both of us no matter whose name the car was titled in. So, I faithfully paid for one-half of the car payments for five years until the loan was paid in full, and I also paid for one-half of all of the other car-related expenses because I trusted him.

We also used my credit card to pay for our trips to Key West, San Francisco, and Fire Island until it was maxed out at $20,000.00. He never paid me back for his expenses but kept promising that he would do so. He would always tell me, "Take a chill pill, Tom, and don't worry about it. Trust me!"

Recently, I discovered that my boyfriend had taken

up cross-dressing and was going to a local transvestite bar and performing on stage as hootchy-cootchy girl. That was the last straw! I confronted him about his new sources of income, and he admitted that he was having a big time and wanted me to dress up as a Yam Queen or Dolly Parton and come to the bar with him. I told him in no uncertain terms that I was not going to put on a dress nor was I going to have a boy friend who wore dresses and sported fake cleavages.

So, that was the end of our relationship.

However, my boyfriend took the car and refused to pay me any money for it. He said that the car was in his name alone and that I was not entitled to anything involving the car. He also refused to pay for any of my credit card bill despite the fact that at least half of the bills on it were for his vacation expenses. When I asked him to pay for his expenses on this credit card bill, he said that the credit card was in my name alone and that it was my problem, not his!

I am not going to take this lying down! What can I do to get my ex-boyfriend to pay me for one-half of the value of the car and for his expenses on my $20,000.00 credit card bill?

ANSWER: In North Carolina, you can file a law suit against Mr. Hootchy-Cootchy and ask the Court to order that he pay you for one-half of the value of the car at the date of separation and for the actual expenses that were charged on his behalf on your credit card.

The Court can crack the financial whip on Mr. Hootchy-Cootchy under theories of contract and unjust enrichment.

Under the law of contracts, you can tell the Court

about the promises that Mr. Hootchy-Cootchy made to you about you being entitled to one-half of the ownership of the car because you paid one-half of the car loan and the car's expenses. You should also argue that Mr. Hootchy-Cootchy should have to pay for his expenses on your credit card because he had promised you to pay them during your relationship.

While Mr. Hootchy-Cootchy made only oral contracts with you, these oral agreements were still made and you relied on them when you spent your money. It will be up to the Court to decide who is telling the truth and what should be done to resolve the situation.

You could also argue that Mr. Hootchy-Cootchy was unjustly enriched by getting all of the car which you helped pay for and by not having to pay back his vacation expenses because the credit card was in your name alone. In order to claim unjust enrichment, you must show that Mr. Hootchy-Cootchy was unfairly enriched by you during your relationship. Given the facts, you should be able to do that if you can show proof of your car payments and car expenses and proof of Mr. Hootchy-Cootchy's expenses on your credit card.

If you are serious about getting your money back, you will need to act now and get a lawyer to file suit against Mr. Hootchy-Cootchy who will never pay you without something being squeezed.

In any relationship that you have in the future, it would be a smart thing to have a written and signed contract between you and your boyfriend if you decide to buy any large ticket item or if he wants to charge things on your credit card. The Court is far more strict about enforcing written contracts than about enforcing oral agreements.

As for men in dresses, they can certainly be deceiving, but please note that none of them can hold a candle to Mel Gibson in a kilt.

# WHEN YOU LAY DOWN WITH DOGS, YOU GET FLEAS

**October 4**

Why I started going out with the scrawny little weirdo in the trailer next to mine, I'll never know, but I did. He was strange but attentive, so I thought, "Why not?". What a mistake!

I always ended paying for our big nights out to go bowling or to our local karaoke bar because he was usually out of a job or had conveniently left his wallet at home. What he liked best was to come to my house for dinner so that I could cook him fried chicken, collards, and potato salad with banana pudding for dessert. Then, he would burp a lot and fall asleep on the sofa with my dog.

That got old.

After about three months of being on the paying/cooking detail, I ended the relationship or whatever it was we had between us, or so I thought.

After we broke up, I began to notice that many times when I got home from work, my TV was on a different channel from where I had left it and six or seven beers and a lot of my leftovers were gone from my refrigerator. Every morning, I made sure that my doors and my windows were locked, but these strange things kept happening. I couldn't figure out how someone could break into my trailer because I was sure that my big dog would bite anyone who tried to get in.

I called the manager of the mobile home park where I live, and told her about the problem, and that is how we found out what was going on.

One morning after I had left for work, my manager parked her car in another nearby lot and started watching my trailer. About an hour after I had left, my scrawny ex-boy friend left his trailer, walked over to my front door, knelt down, and crawled through the dog door at the bottom of my front door.

My manager called the police, and when they arrived at my trailer, they found him sitting on my sofa with my dog, watching my TV, drinking my beer, eating my leftovers, and feeding my dog treats to my dog!

Of course, he was arrested for a bunch of things, and I had hoped that wearing orange for a little while would learn him to leave me and my stuff alone, but it hasn't. Now, my ex-boy friend is calling me all the time saying that he misses me, my dog, and my fried chicken. I told him that my frying days for him are over and to not call me anymore, but he pays it no mind.

What can I do to stop him from calling me at least twenty times a day because it is really starting to upset and bother me?


ANSWER:  There are a number of things that you can do to keep Mr. Dog Door at bay.

First, you should call Mr. Dog Door's probation officer, if he has one, and let him know that Mr. Dog Door is continuing to harass you by repeatedly calling you and that you want to have Mr. Dog Door back in jail for violating the terms of his probation.

Next, you should go to the magistrate and file criminal charges for harassing phone calls against Mr. Dog Door and ask that as a condition of his bond, he be required to not call or contact you in any way pending a trial on this charge.

You could also file a domestic violence complaint against him based on the fact that his breaking into your house and his continued harassment of you has inflicted substantial emotional distress on you. Ask the court to order that he not contact you in any way or come into your house. Call the Carteret County Domestic Violence office, and they can help you with this complaint.

Finally, you could get caller ID and stop answering the phone when you see that Mr. Dog Door is calling you for another free meal. You don't need to listen to Mr. Dog Door's lament of unrequited love and need for fried chicken unless you want to do so.

So, you do need to do something to curb Mr. Dog Door's bad behavior because it is often true that weird people's behavior can get weirder if they do not have some strong consequences for their bad behavior. Unless you do something, Mr. Dog Door will not stop calling you.

Take action with some or all of the things outlined above and make sure that Mr. Dog Door begins to understand that your bark is every bit as bad as your bite.

# WHEN MOM SHACKS UP, SHOULD THE KIDS SHIP OUT?

**October 11**

When I came home one evening and saw my clothes hanging from all the bushes and trees in our front yard, it was clear that my wife had gotten mad at me and had thrown pretty much everything that I owned out of our second story bedroom window. After she also slammed the front door in my face and changed the locks, I figured correctly that our marriage was over.

Since we had three kids, I tried to be reasonable, and we worked it out in a court order so that we had joint legal custody of the kids, and she had the kids most of the time while I had them every other weekend.

She stayed in our house with the kids until the lease ran out, and then, she shocked me when she took herself and my three kids and moved in with her unemployed, dirt bag boyfriend in his two bedroom trailer in Otway. He has custody of his one kid, and now, all four kids are sleeping in two bunk beds in one of the bedrooms. Sometimes, my kids sleep on the sofa in the living room or on an air mattress on the floor.

I told her that I did not think that was a good situation for our kids to be in and that it wasn't good for them to see their mother living in sin and they shouldn't be crammed into that den of iniquity and fornication like sardines. She said that I needed to mind my own business or else go to hell. There didn't seem to be too much for me to say to her after that.

Except for me, my ex-wife's choices in men have ranged from bad to worse, and this latest misstep is just further evidence of her bad taste in men.

Since my ex-wife is being a very poor role model for our children, I want to get primary custody of our children and get them out of this terrible situation. What do I have to do to get my kids away from my ex-wife and her harlot ways?

ANSWER: In North Carolina, you must prove a substantial change of circumstances which are adversely or positively affecting the minor children before you can successfully get the Court to change custody from Ms. Harlot to you. In other words, you must find actual evidence that your children are being harmed by the change in their living situation.

So, you need to talk to your children's teachers to see if they notice any change for worse in your children's behavior in class. Get copies of the children's report cards and see if their grades are going down and if they are having an increased number of tardies and unexcused absences from school.

You could also take your children to a counselor or ask the school counselor talk to them about whether or not this change in their home is bothering them. If the children talk to a counselor, that counselor could be an expert witness for you in court if the children report that they are not happy with their current living arrangement.

Talking to your kids to see how they like living in a bunk bed infested bedroom would also be a good idea. You also need to know how your children feel about Mr. Dirt bag, his child, and his two bedroom trailer.

You should also do a little research on Mr. Dirt bag by having a private investigator run a state and federal criminal record check on him. If he has any pending criminal charges or prior criminal convictions during the last ten years, you want to know all about it.

This same private investigator could also be helpful to you in documenting what goes on in Ms. Harlot's household on the weekends that she has the kids. You might find out that Mr. Dirt bag has highly lucrative and illegal sources of income that you had not previously known about. You might also find out that Ms. Harlot leaves the kids alone in the trailer for extended periods of time or else has wide open parties with lots of alcohol and drugs at the trailer when the kids are at home.

Additionally, you need to hire a family law attorney who can put all of this information together for you in a motion to modify primary physical custody from Ms. Harlot to you. The key thing here is that you must prove that the change is substantial from the date that the last custody order was entered and that this change is adversely affecting your children.

The Court will not assume that it is harmful for your children to live with their mother's boyfriend without actual proof of this harm. So, you need to get this evidence together and come to court loaded for bear.

Don't tell Ms. Harlot what you are up to since the

element of surprise will definitely work in your favor. You need to gather this information quickly and file your motion as soon as possible so that your children can hopefully be removed from this harmful environment in a short period of time.

Don't give up because your children deserve to grow up in a family situation that is based on virtue and common sense rather than one based on selfishness and run-amok hormones.

# THE STUD CLUB

### October 18

It all started when I began to notice a lot of expensive, specially made leather goods being charged on our credit card and when my husband of 25 years stayed gone most every Saturday afternoon. After about two months of this stuff, I confronted him and asked him what was going on.

In response, my husband gave a little smile and said, "Well, why don't you come with me this weekend." So, I did.

The next Saturday, we drove way out in the country and down a long dirt road to a big barn in the middle of nowhere. There were a lot of cars parked around the barn, but I didn't see anyone outside. After we parked, we went to a small barn door which had a small sign on it saying "The Stud Club". My husband gave a special type of knock, and then the door opened.

Once inside, I could not believe what I was seeing. Here were about 25 grown men and women all running around buck nekkid and acting like horses. They were neighing and prancing and jumping around like a bunch of lunatics. Even worse, some of the people had bridles and saddles on and were being led by their "trainers".

Frankly, I had never seen or even remotely imagined anything as bizarre as what was going on before me. I didn't think it could get any worse until I saw my husband.

While I had been staring with my mouth open at all these goings on, my husband had slipped into a little stall. He came running out naked as a jay bird but wearing a little leather bridle and a baseball hat which said "#1 Stud". He looked at me with this big grin on his face and said, "Well, isn't it great? What do you think?"

For once, I couldn't think of anything to say. My husband was apparently relieved because he went on to explain how The Stud Club worked. It wasn't just all nekkid prancing around. Oh no! After a little "warm up" time, the "stallions" would pick out the "mares" that they liked, and they would proceed to do the wild thing right then and there. Then, it was time for more prancing around and after that, it was time to change your partner and do it again.

After this explanation, my husband handed me a bridle and said, "Come on, honey! Why don't you get ready to saddle up!"

Hell flew in me! I threw that bridle on the ground and stormed out of there. I got into our truck and roared off down the road with my buck nekkid husband running after me waving his arms and yelling.

How he got home, I do not know, but when he did, I told him in no uncertain terms that our marriage was over and that he had to get out of the house. My husband told me that he didn't have a problem with the fact that he was out having "fun" at The Stud Club every weekend, and if I minded his "hobby", well, that was just my problem, and he was not moving out.

Now, my husband and I are sleeping in separate bedrooms, and he is still going to The Stud Club every Saturday afternoon. He will not move out, and I cannot afford to because I make very little money at my part-time job and he makes a lot of money as the owner of a construction company.

This whole situation is driving me crazy! My husband is trying to make me think that my objections to his participation in The Stud Club are stupid and that he should be able to continue with his "hobby". Just the thought of him standing there wearing that bridle and that stupid baseball cap makes me want to laugh hysterically and then punch him in the nose.

How can I get him and his "riding equipment" out of the house now?


ANSWER:  The naked fact of the matter is that Mr. Stud's participation in The Stud Club is not a hobby, but is instead adultery. He is being unfaithful to you with other women, and you do not have to put up with that kind of behavior.

In North Carolina, you can file suit and ask the Court to grant you something called a divorce from bed and board. This is not a regular divorce which you cannot get until you have been separated from Mr. Stud for at least one year. Instead, a divorce from bed and board is sort of a court-ordered legal separation.

In order to get a divorce from bed and board, you have to allege and prove particular types of marital misconduct committed by your spouse. Adultery is one of these kinds of misconduct which can be the basis for a divorce from bed and board.

Also as part of a divorce from bed and board, the Court can order that you get possession of the marital residence and that Mr. Stud has to get out. The Court can also order that a supporting spouse like Mr. Stud must pay a dependent spouse like you post-separation support on a regular basis.

So, you need to hire a private investigator to get evidence of your husband's adultery and to document your husband's bareback riding at The Stud Club.

You should also look around the house and find all of the "riding equipment" and that baseball cap to use as evidence in court if Mr. Stud is foolish enough to want a truly memorable hearing on this matter. Take the bridles, saddles, hat, and whatever else you find and put them in a safe place to use at a later date if necessary.

It would also be useful to have all the credit card receipts for the "riding equipment" that Mr. Stud has purchased since you can also use that as some really great evidence should you need to go to court for a hearing.

Finally, you need a good family law attorney who can put the hooves to Mr. Stud and crack the whip too.

Get going and don't delay. Mr. Stud's behavior is off the charts and unacceptable. Mr. Stud needs to learn that if he wants to play "horsie", he is going to have to pay the piper and you.

# YOU CAN'T OUTSTINK A SKUNK

### October 25

My granddaughter is everything to me. She is now four years old, and she and I have a special bond because of all the hard times that we went through together.

These hard times started when my daughter, mother of my granddaughter, married a successful businessman who is a combination of a rat and a skunk. Shortly after my granddaughter's third birthday, her father took off with another woman and left my daughter and my granddaughter flat.

Since my daughter had no job and no money of her own, she and my granddaughter moved back in with me for six months. During that time, she found a job and I cared for my granddaughter. My granddaughter and I had a great time together, and I was happy that my daughter was no longer with her jerk of a husband.

Unfortunately, I told my daughter what I thought of her husband in no uncertain terms, and she did not forget anything that I said. When she would complain that her husband was always saying ugly things to her and trying to pick a fight, I would tell her to not respond in kind to him because you can't outstink a skunk.

Her husband would not pay child support and kept threatening to take the child, so I gave my daughter some money for an attorney who filed suit against her husband for a bunch of things including custody. They went to mediation and agreed on how to share custody and that I would have grandparent visitation rights of one weekend a month with my granddaughter. This agreement was put into a court order.

Then, out of the blue and with her husband's promise of a new SUV for her, my daughter reconciled with her husband. She quit her job, took my granddaughter, and moved back in with her husband. However, they never dismissed their law suit against each other.

It wasn't long before my daughter had told her husband all the nasty things that I had said about him. He was very angry with me and decided that I was trying to break up his marriage to my daughter. As a punishment for my critical remarks about him, he told me that I could no longer see my granddaughter. My spineless daughter went along with all this, and now, I have not been able to see my granddaughter for the last two months.

What can I do to see my granddaughter? Do I have any rights as a grandparent?

ANSWER: In North Carolina, parents who are not separated from each other have the right to control who their children may associate with, and that includes whether or not the children will have any contact with their grandparents.

The only exception to this rule is where the parents were previously separated and there was a court order granting visitation or custody to one or more of the grandparents.  Where there has been a prior court order giving a grandparent visitation with or custody of the grandchildren, that grandparent has the right to go back to court and ask the court to continue that visitation or custody.

In your case, you happily have a court order granting you one weekend a month visitation with your grand-daughter.  So, you need to get a good family law attorney and go back to court to ask that the terms of this order be enforced so that you can get your court-ordered visitation with your granddaughter.

Be happy that you have this court-ordered visitation because if you did not, your daughter and Mr. Skunk could legally prevent you from seeing your granddaughter and there would be nothing that you could do about it.

In addition to all the legal fireworks, you might try talking to your daughter and Mr. Skunk and apologizing for your remarks.  You could also offer to care for the child when your daughter and Mr. Skunk want to go out or help pay for your granddaughter's clothes or other expenses.  In other words, bribe your way back into your granddaughter's life.

You should do whatever it takes to see your grand-daughter.  What you should not do is make any more negative comments about Mr. Skunk to your daughter or granddaughter.

Smile sweetly at Mr. & Mrs. Skunk and work through the court and outside of it to see your granddaugh-ter.  Your granddaughter is going to need you dearly in the years to come, and you need to be there to help her grow up to be a young lady with a spine and not a skunk.

# THE SHOOT-OUT AT THE NO-TELL MOTEL

### November 1

When my husband of thirty years started coming home late from work with a guilty yet satisfied look on his face, I began to look at his comings and goings with a little more interest.

It was when I found a picture of a much younger woman in his wallet that I decided to hire a private investigator or PI to find out just what was going on.

On several different occasions, the PI followed my husband after he left from work, but my husband somehow always managed to elude the PI until my husband returned home two hours later apologetic yet smiling all the while.

So without telling the PI, I decided to help the PI by following him following my husband. Then, if the PI lost the scent of the hunt, I would be there to pick it up and follow my husband to where his call of the wild was leading him.

One fateful evening, my husband left work and got into his middle-age crisis car, a red Corvette, and roared off down the road with my PI on his tail. I eased out my white mini-van from the next block and took off in hot pursuit.

I had to run a few "pink" (not quite red) lights and keep my pedal to the metal, but I finally saw my husband pull up to a curb and pick up this much younger cheap piece of goods who was waiting there to meet him. This brazen hussy had dyed blonde hair, lots of make-up, obvious implants, a very low blouse and a very short skirt. What my husband could see in such a tramp, I do not know.

They sat in the car necking until somebody blew their horn at them, and then, my husband burned rubber and raced down the road like he was going to a house on fire.

When I finally caught up with him, his car was parked in front of a room at our local "No-Tell Motel" right in line with all of the other middle-age crisis cars in front of their rooms. My PI was parked across the parking lot, and I could see that he was sitting in his car video-taping this event. I parked across the street because I didn't want my husband or my PI to see me. I sat there and watched for about an hour. As I imagined what was going on in that flea bag motel room, hell flew in me and I got out of the car.

Now, I have a trusty 38 revolver called "Betsy" that I had in my purse, and I thought that I had a good plan to get my husband and his shameless hussy out of the motel room so that I could prove what my husband had been up to.

I ran in front of that motel room and yelled in my loudest voice, "I KNOW THAT YOU ARE IN THERE WITH MY HUSBAND! COME OUT NOW WITH YOUR HANDS UP OR I'LL START SHOOTING!". Then, I fired off Betsy with three or four warning shots over the roof of the motel just to get their attention.

It was quiet for about 30 seconds. Then, doors burst open all up and down that No-Tell Motel as about twenty men and women in various stages of undress shot out of their rooms, dove into their cars, and raced and jockeyed for position to get out of the motel parking lot. None of them turned on their car lights but I could hear lots of cussing and yelling.

Then, I saw my husband dressed only in his BVD's with his hussy wrapped in a blanket sprint for his car. I fired up old Betsy and put a few shots over their heads just to see how fast I could make them run. Pretty fast, as it turned out.

While I was reloading, my PI ran up and took away my gun. We watched as all the cars left the parking lot at about 80 miles per hour and then accelerated when they reached the road until they were out of sight.

I was fired up and wanted to follow them, but my PI said "No, I think that you have done quite enough for one evening." He then advised me to get the hell out of there before the police arrived, so we left.

So now, I have my PI's videotape of my husband and his cheap slut at the No-Tell Motel and them running undressed to his car. Is that enough evidence to prove my husband's adultery? If not, what kind of evidence do I need to prove my husband's adultery?

ANSWER: The good news is that you have enough evidence on the video tape to prove your husband's adultery but the bad news is that there is probably also enough evidence on the videotape to have you criminally charged with carrying a concealed weapon, assault with a deadly weapon, and going armed to the terror of the people.  And that is just for starters.

However, back to your question.

In North Carolina, you must prove that your husband was inclined to commit adultery and then, had the opportunity to do so.  Here, your husband showed his inclination to commit adultery by kissing Ms. Cheap Slut in his car, by going with her to the No-Tell Motel, and later, by running out of the motel in his BVD's with Ms. Cheap Slut wrapped in a blanket.

Your husband also obviously showed that he had the opportunity to commit adultery by being in the motel room with Ms. Cheap Slut for at least one hour which would probably be more than enough time for him to achieve mission accomplished.

Also, you have the testimony of the PI who can verify and document all of your husband's philandering and adulterous behavior on that fateful evening.  Unfortunately, this PI can also probably verify and document all of your criminal behavior with ol' Betsy.  So, this PI's testimony and videotape are double edged swords.

You need to talk to a good family law attorney as soon as possible to figure out what you need to do next in the dissolution of your marriage.  In the meantime, it is important that you and Betsy stay home and do not follow the PI or your husband or Ms. Cheap Slut on any more high speed chases or engage in any more Wild West shoot outs.

Let your PI and your attorney take aim at your husband and Ms. Cheap Slut, not you and ol' Betsy.

# FISHING FOR TROUT AND CATCHING A TOAD FISH

**November 8**

All this trouble began in May when I came from my home in Raleigh to Morehead City for a fishing tournament with three of my fishing buddies. We went to one of the parties sponsored by the tournament, and there, I met this very pretty local girl from Newport.

That night, she and I ate, drank, and were merry. Very merry as a matter of fact because she spent the night with me in my hotel room. Since I am not married, I was delighted to make her acquaintance, and we continued to get to know each other better and better in my hotel room during the week that I was in Morehead City.

After I got back to Raleigh, we continued the romance, and usually she would come to Raleigh for an occasional weekend, and once, she and I stayed at my motel room at Atlantic Beach for a few days. I never went to her house, but it seemed that was only because the opportunity never presented itself. We were just having a great time together but the relationship was not serious.

Then in October, a sheriff's deputy knocked on my

door and handed me some legal documents which said that a Marine Corps officer was suing me for criminal conversation with his wife.  At first, I thought that he was accusing me of having some heavy breathing, nasty talking phone calls with his wife.  Then, I realized that the sweet thang that I had been seeing was his wife, and he had been overseas on duty during the time she and I had been together having a big time.

Now, she had never mentioned one word about being married and having a husband.  I was completely astonished because I would never have gone out with her had I known that she was married.

These legal papers accused me of having sexual intercourse with his wife during the time that they were married, and he wants me to pay him a lot of money for his loss of her services in the home, emotional distress, humiliation, and mental anguish due to our romantic relationship.  I can't believe that I would have to pay anything since I did not know that she was married.

She deceived me, and I should not have to pay for this deception.  What should I do?

ANSWER:  Unfortunately for you, North Carolina is one of the few states which still has the old fashioned legal remedy of criminal conversation.  In order to sue you for criminal conversation, the Marine must only prove that he was married to Ms. Deceiver and that you had sexual intercourse with her during the time that he was married to her.

Criminal conversation is a strict liability tort which means that it doesn't matter that you didn't know that Ms. Deceiver was married.  All that matters is that Ms. Deceiver was married to the Marine and that you had sexual intercourse with her during the time that she was married to him.

So, the Marine can sue you for criminal conversation and ask the court to award him damages for loss of services in the home, emotional distress, humiliation, and mental anguish. How much he will be awarded in damages from you is anybody's guess, but he is clearly entitled to sue you for criminal conversation with Ms. Deceiver.

You need to immediately stop all contact with Ms. Deceiver and hire an attorney right away to defend you in this law suit. In the future, it would be wise to ask all future flings if they are married and to check around a little more if the flings say "no" to that question. Also, you might want to fish more and troll less at the next fishing tournament you attend.

# SHRIMPING MERCIES

**November 15**

My wife is from Otway, and she can cuss the ears off a brass monkey. Last week, she gave me a cussing the likes of which I have never had before. My ears are still ringing. Here is what happened.

Now, I am from West Virginia and while I have done a lot of white water kayaking, I have never been to the ocean except once as a little kid. But I love the water, and it was sort of fate that I met my wife, married her, and moved to Otway.

I met my wife at a NASCAR race, and we had both been drinking plenty of beer to keep up our fluids because it was so hot out. When I saw her bottle blonde hair, butterfly tattoo and body piercing in sort of a blurry way, it was love at first sight. I knew that I had to make her mine.

So, we went out, and I soon discovered that she had even more amazing tattoos and body piercings in the most unbelievable places. After a couple of months, we got married, and I moved into her trailer in Otway.

A couple of times, her uncles and cousins took me out shrimping with them on Core Sound, and I loved it. I really admired the Down East watermen that I met, and I just sort of wanted to be like them, so I bought a shrimp boat.

I called my boat after my wife's name, the "Hattie Coll". My wife was named "Hattie Coll" after the wonderful drops that her mother took on a regular basis all her life for her nerves. I had hoped that owning a shrimp boat would be as soothing to me as the drops were for her, but I was wrong.

Last week, one of my hunting buddies from West Virginia came down to visit me, and after quite a few beers, we decided that we would take the Hattie Coll out shrimping on her maiden voyage the next morning.

In the morning when we woke up, it was blowing hard and there were a lot of whitecaps out in Back Bay, but we figured that we could handle it because we were used to some pretty serious white water in West Virginia, and we agreed that the ocean was just like white water, only a little bigger.

So, we got in the Hattie Coll and took her out to the Beaufort Inlet. As we were going out the inlet into the ocean, the wind was blowing even harder and the waves were pretty big. My friend, Bubba, wanted to know why there weren't any other boats out except us. I told him that I had no idea but that I was glad we were the only ones out there because that way, we would get all the shrimp.

We had no more made it out the inlet when the steering on the Hattie Coll broke, and all of a sudden, I couldn't steer the boat. As the waves poured into the boat, Bubba started bailing hard and fast while I found the broken cable and worked as quick as I could to fix it. Bubba hollered at me that maybe we should call the Coast Guard which I told him was probably a good idea except that I didn't have a radio on the Hattie Coll and I had forgot to bring my cell phone.

So, he bailed like crazy, and I luckily fixed the steering cable in pretty short order so I was finally able to steer the boat into the waves.  We were back in the shrimping business!

As I started to get ready to put the net out, more disaster struck.  The boat's engine just stopped, and once again, the waves started pouring into the boat.  By then, Bubba knew the drill, so he started bailing like a madman.  I ran over to the engine and started to mess with it and all those wires.

Over the roar of the wind and waves, Bubba yelled at me that maybe it would be a good idea to put on some life jackets.  I hollered back that it probably would be a good idea except I didn't know where the life jackets were on my boat.

I could hear Bubba cussing, and then, I somehow started the engine and I hollered to him that now we would get some great shrimp for him to take back to West Virginia.

As I lowered the net, a huge wave appeared and crashed over the boat.  In a second, I was washed overboard and just missed the net.  I started swimming as fast as I could, but I just couldn't swim faster than the current.  I could see Bubba yelling at me, but I started swallowing a lot of water and couldn't seem to swim as fast because the water was so cold.

Just then, another big wave picked me up and threw me by the net.  I grabbed onto it and somehow, I managed to get back into the boat.  As I lay on the floor of the boat gasping and choking and trying to sit up, Bubba looked up and said to me, "Why is there all that white water just over there?"

I sat up and looked. It was the Fort Macon jetty with huge waves hitting it and shooting up into the air! We were headed straight for it!

I grabbed the wheel and somehow got past the jetty back into Beaufort Inlet. Then, Bubba, who was a pale shade of green, looked at me and said that he thought that it would be a good idea if we called it a day and went shrimping some other time. I agreed with him, got the net up and headed back to Beaufort.

As we went under the drawbridge, I yelled at Bubba not to worry because we were almost at the dock. Unfortunately, the words were no sooner out of my mouth when the net caught on one of the pilings around the bridge. We were stuck!

So, with the bridge open, all traffic stopped, and lots of waves bouncing us up and down, I had to try and get the net untangled from the piling. It took a while and Bubba had to hang himself over the rail from time to time and call the Irish, but I finally got us untangled and underway.

We made it back to the dock without any more problems except that we didn't get any shrimp because I had forgotten to tie the bag off.

As Bubba crawled out of the Hattie Coll onto the dock, he told me that he was going to stick with Class VI whitewater, and that from now on, he would buy any shrimp that he wanted to eat.

So, I went home and told my wife about my first shrimping adventure. She looked at me and started cussing. The gist of it was that I was dumb as a conch, that my parentage was uncertain, that I needed to learn what a gale warning meant, and that I could only go shrimping on the Hattie Coll again if I took out $100,000.00 in life insurance and named her as the beneficiary.

She also wanted me to make a will and name her as my sole heir. I think that wills are bad luck, and so, I don't want to write a will. Besides, I have a son who is now 15 and lives with his mama, who is my cousin and was my first wife, in West Virginia, and I want to leave him something too.

I am not going to write a will, so I need to know how my wife and my son would divide up my estate if I didn't have a will and I had bought the farm on my first shrimping expedition.

ANSWER: Before you do anything else, you need to get down on your knees and thank Jesus for giving you shrimping mercies. Only the Hand of God could have saved you that day from yourself, and He did just that.

As for your question, North Carolina law states that if you die without a will and you have a wife and one child, your wife would get 50% and your son would get 50% of all real estate owned by you. As for your personal property, your wife would get all of your personal property up to the first $30,000.00, but your wife and your son would each get 50% of your personal property worth over that first $30,000.00.

So, your son would be able inherit something from you if you had enough assets even if you did not have a will when you died.

Besides the will issue, you need to think seriously about learning from your wife's family about shrimping, boats, and the ocean before you give Death another shot at you out on the water. It would be good to prove to your wife that you are not dumb as a conch so that your brass monkey could keep its ears on for a while.

# DON'T FEED STRAY DOGS

### November 29

At first, I sort of liked this guy at work. He was a little weird, but he really seemed to like me. When he asked me out, I told him that I couldn't because I had just gotten out of an abusive relationship, and I wanted a little time off.

That didn't slow him down much. He always comes over to my desk and talks to me a lot, and his little weird ways are getting a lot weirder.

Last week, he asked me to come down to his truck in the office parking lot because he wanted to show me something. During my break, I went with him, and he opened up his truck's glove box and started showing me his new hand gun. It was big and black, and he demonstrated its "speed loader" or something like that and talked a lot about how powerful and fast his gun was.

Just the way he looked and the way he kept rubbing his hands all over his gun made me uncomfortable. I told him that his gun was very nice but that I had to get back to work, and then I took off back into our office building.

Over this last weekend, I had made a sweet potato pie, so I brought him some, and he liked it a lot. Every day this week, he has asked me out, and I have kept telling him no, but he is getting angrier with me each time I refuse to go out with him. I am beginning to be a little afraid of him.

When I told my brother about this situation, he said to me, "Baby doll, now that you have fed him, you are going to have a hard time getting rid of him. Also, when a man shows you his gun, it's the same thing as him showing you his Johnson."

He told me to stop feeding this stray dog and to not let him show me anything else.

I don't know what to do. This guy is kind of cute, but he is very aggressive and starting to give me the creeps. I want him to stop asking me out, but I don't want him angry with me. What should I do?

ANSWER: For starters, you need to stop sending mixed messages to Mr. Stray Dog who is, by your own description, weird, aggressive, and has a gun that he likes to fondle a lot.

You need to tell him in no uncertain terms that you do not want to go out with him. Say it plainly but kindly, and don't beat around the bush. Then, stay away from him. No more going someplace with him for Show and Tell. No more little home-made baked treats for Mr. Stray Dog. No more chatty chats at work.

If you are firm in your rejection, Mr. Stray Dog may start to sniff around somewhere else. If he doesn't move on to another target, you should have a conversation with your supervisor about Mr. Stray Dog's unwanted attentions at work, and your supervisor should be able to tell Mr. Stray Dog in terms that he will understand that his intentions towards you need to be stifled immediately.

Should Mr. Stray Dog persist, you can take legal action through a special type of restraining order to keep him at bay and away from you. However, you should get a good family law attorney to file this law suit for you, and this legal step should be the last resort and the final silver bullet in your rejection of his advances towards you.

Finally, you should start to see a counselor and find out why you are attracted to abusive, weird guys, and why they are attracted to you. You appear to be like a moth to a flame where abusive, weird relationships are concerned. As you go from one bad affair to the next, you are just going from the frying pan to the fire. It would be a very good thing for you to stop all of that before you get hurt in more ways than one.

So, tell Mr. Stray Dog to move it on down the road and show his piece to someone else. Then, stick to your guns and get some counseling to help you start rejecting the stray dogs and start choosing the show dogs.

# EVERY MOMENT IN THE SUN
# HAS ITS COST

### December 6

About a year ago, I had this sort-of girlfriend who lives in Ernul and who came to spend the night with me a couple of times here in Newport. We met at a bar over on the beach, and I liked her fine but it was nothing special.

When she told me that she was pregnant and thought that I was the father, I told her to forget that stuff and didn't call her again. She didn't call me either so I thought that trouble had passed me by. I was wrong.

Two months ago, I got served with a law suit naming me as the father of my ex-sort-of girlfriend's baby girl. The law suit asked the court to order that I pay a huge amount of child support for 18 years and health insurance for the kid, and, to add insult to injury, that I be required to pay all of the medical expenses for my ex-sort-of girlfriend's pregnancy and the kid's birth. It is a lot of money, and I don't want to pay it.

So, I went to court last month, and my lawyer asked the court to order genetic testing on me, my ex-sort-of girlfriend, and the baby to see if this kid is mine, and the court did do that. When the lab report came back, I was found to be 98.9999% Daddy to this baby. What a bummer!

The court then ordered me to pay for all of the medical expenses for my ex-sort-of girlfriend's pregnancy and birth of the kid and a rip off amount of child support every month that will be taken automatically out of my paycheck so that it will now be hard for me to make my truck and jet ski payments. To pour salt in the wound, the court also ordered me to pay for the genetic testing and back child support from the date that the law suit was filed and to provide health insurance for the kid.

This is breaking me financially, and I will probably have to sell my jet ski to pay for this kid and all of her costs.

When she spent the night, my ex-sort-of girlfriend told me that she was on the pill, so I didn't worry about birth control. As it turns out, she wasn't on the pill at all. She just tricked me into getting her pregnant! This whole thing is not fair!

How can I get out of paying for these medical expenses, the paternity test costs, the kid's health insurance, and child support?


ANSWER: The only way out of paying these costs is to die, and even then, your estate would have to pay the outstanding court-ordered costs for the medical expenses, paternity test, and back child support that you owed when you died.

So, if you are breathing, you are paying. There is no way out.

You could have avoided all of this procreative expense by you being the one responsible for birth control. A box of condoms would have cost a whole lot less than what you are now going to pay for the next 18 years.

You fathered a child, and your child has the right to be supported by you. So, sell the jet ski, pay your court-ordered expenses, and be grateful that your ex-sort-of girlfriend didn't have twins.

Also, as the father of this child, you should now think about how you can be a good father to your daughter. She needs you to act like her father and not just a sperm donor. For her sake and yours as well, step up to the plate, pay your child support, and be a good Daddy to your little girl.

# THE NAKED CHRISTMAS TREE DANCE

**December 13**

If it had not been for a Moonlight Madness Sale, I would never have discovered my husband's secret and witnessed his strange behavior.

Last week, I had finished decorating the house and our nine foot Christmas tree and had decided to go Christmas shopping that evening at our local department store's Moonlight Madness Sale. I got my Christmas lists together and said goodbye to my husband of thirty years who was sitting in his barcolounger, drinking scotch, and watching TV just like he does every evening.

I drove off down the road, and was well on my way to town when I realized that I had forgotten my wallet with all of my credit cards. So, there was nothing else to do but turn around and go back home and get the plastic.

When I walked in the house, I got the shock of my life. There, by the Christmas tree, was my husband holding a bottle of scotch and dancing around the tree stark naked except for a red Santa hat and a strategically placed large red bow.

Gasping for air, I asked him what in the Sam Hill he was doing. He then told me that he was doing his annual

Naked Christmas Tree Dance which was something that he did every year because he felt that it was liberating and helped him get into the Christmas spirit. He then raised his scotch bottle in salute at me and started to hop around the tree while singing "Deck the Halls" in a very slurred fashion.

I told him that he needed to pull himself together right away and close the drapes because he didn't need to upset the neighbors and scare the children with his in-the-buff performance. My husband refused to get dressed or close the drapes. In fact, he pranced right up to me and loudly announced, "Look at that! Santa has brought you a big candy cane for Christmas!"

I told him in no uncertain terms that I was not going to put up with his foolishness and that I was not going to miss the Moonlight Madness Sale because of it and that I was going to town right then and there. My husband took another swig from his bottle and told me to suit myself. Then, he started to dance around the tree singing Jingle Bells.

I left and went shopping, but I am now having very serious concerns about my husband's sanity. I want him to see a doctor because I think that he needs a shot or something. My husband refuses to go to the doctor and says that the only shot that he needs is another shot of scotch.

Can I make my husband go to the doctor so that he can check out my husband and do something about my husband's inappropriate behavior.

ANSWER: The only way that you can force your husband to see a doctor is if you have him involuntarily committed at a hospital. In order to have your husband involuntarily committed, you would have to go to a magistrate or a clerk of court, give him or her an affidavit in which you describe your husband's behavior and your concerns, and then, convince that person that your husband is a threat to himself or others.

If the magistrate or clerk of court finds that it is likely that your husband is a threat to himself or others, he or she can issue an order that a law enforcement official or other authorized person can take your husband into custody for examination by a physician or eligible psychologist. Your husband can then be held for 24 hours while he undergoes psychological testing at a hospital authorized to do this testing.

If the treating physician or psychiatrist does not find that your husband is a threat to himself or others, your husband will be released and the proceeding is at an end.

If the treating physician or psychiatrist does find that your husband is a threat to himself or others, your husband can be kept at the hospital, but a hearing in court will be held within 10 days of your husband being taken into custody.

So, what this all means is that you will probably have World War III on your hands if you try to have your husband committed.

You might talk to your husband's primary physician about this unusual behavior and see what he recommends, but don't hold your breath about changing your husband's behavior.

Your husband does not sound as if he is a threat to himself or others. He sounds as if he is a man who is a little eccentric and who likes to show off his candy cane.

So, you might leave well enough alone and just close

the drapes if you leave home at night to go somewhere. Or you could give your husband the shock of his life by joining him in the Naked Christmas Tree Dance – just be sure to close the drapes before you do.

# DO UNTO OTHERS

## December 20

All I want is my court-ordered rights as a parent! No more, no less!  But my ex-husband thinks that he can waltz in here and ask for more time with my 7 year old son on Christmas Day, of all days!  He also thinks that I should give it to him.

Well, no way!  I just know that my son doesn't even want to see him.  I even asked my son if he wouldn't rather stay with me all Christmas vacation rather than see his father some.  In response, my son sort of looked at his feet and mumbled something, but I know that what he said is that he wants to stay with me and doesn't want to see his father at all over Christmas.

My ex-husband is a no-good lying skunk who has made lots of money since we separated.  Earlier this year, he went off and married a much younger trophy wife who only wants him for all his money.  I can see that clearly.

So, my son wants to be with me this Christmas because I love him so much and because he is all that I have in life.  Unlike my ex-husband, I have not remarried because I want to dedicate myself to raising my son.

Well, back to my problem which is really not my problem at all because it is my ex-husband who has the problem. The court order says that I will have my son until 3:00 p.m. on Christmas Day and then, my ex-husband is supposed to pick up my son at 3:00 p.m. and keep him until January 2.

Two weeks ago, my ex-husband called me and asked if he could pick up my son at 1:00 p.m. this year on Christmas Day because his family is having a big get together with all of my son's aunts, uncles, and cousins, and their dinner is going to start at 2:00 p.m. at his grandmother's house. He wanted the earlier pickup time of 1:00 p.m. so that he and my son could be there on time for all of the dinner.

He offered to give me more time on some other holiday, but I told him to forget it! He gets his court-ordered time with my son, and I get my court-ordered time! Tough luck to him if he wants more!

If my ex-husband was still married to me, he could see my son all that he wanted to and he wouldn't be hassling me about changing court-ordered visitation on Christmas Day. But he could not get along with me, so now, he doesn't get to see my son whenever he chooses.

Don't you agree that I am entitled to have my court-ordered rights as a parent and that I don't have to change a thing about the Christmas Day visitation just because my ex-husband asks me to do so?

ANSWER: I think that you are asking the wrong question. I think that you should ask yourself what is best for your child and then ask yourself how you can make those good things happen for him.

In this situation, it would very likely be a good thing

for your son to be with his father's extended family for a big Christmas dinner rather than arriving late after everyone had finished eating. So, why not work with your ex-husband to help him with something that would be beneficial for your child.

As you surely know, the terms of the court order trump either parent's requests for changes in the order. So, you are within your rights to stick to the letter of the court order and keep the times of your son's visitation with your ex-husband as outlined in the court order.

However, you need to think about what you are doing. Are you using your son as your weapon of choice to hurt and antagonize your ex-husband? Are you motivated by bitterness and anger to keep your son away from your ex-husband as much as possible? Are you willing to emotionally destroy your son in order to get back at and revenge yourself upon your ex-husband?

Further, Christmas is not just about presents, Santa Claus, and eggnog. If you are a Christian, it is about love, compassion, forgiveness, and sacrifice. You would set a good example of these virtues to your son if you were to let him go with his father a little earlier this Christmas. Helping your son build a good relationship with his father and his father's family could well be the best gift that you could give your son this Christmas.

# NERVE TONICS AND CHRISTMAS SPIRITS

## December 27

When my wife told me that we were going to her sister's on Christmas Day for her first annual big family get-together and Christmas dinner, I knew that the only way I would make it through the dinner with her wacko family is with a little help from my favorite nerve tonic.

So, I slid a fifth of gin into my coat pocket and headed out the door with my wife to her sister's house in Newport. When we got there, that whole big-mouth crowd was talking as hard and as loud as they could. We were all crammed into a couple of little rooms, and it was hot and stuffy.

Then, we heard the bad news. My sister-in-law had gotten into the cooking sherry and had somehow failed to read the directions right on roasting the turkey. So, when the potatoes, vegetables, and the ham were ready, the turkey still had two hours to cook.

In order to have an adequate attitude adjustment, my brother-in-law and I repeatedly slid off to the garage as the turkey cooked, and we refreshed ourselves with our respective bottles of nerve tonic.

Time passed, and as we imbibed our spirits, the more we were filled with the Christmas spirit. Every time I would go into the house, my wife would squint her beady little eyes at me and come over and ask me what I had been doing. "Getting into the Christmas spirit!", I would sing out sweetly to her with a big grin.

Finally, dinner was ready, and it was a good thing because my bottle of nerve tonic was gone. Unfortunately, I ended up sitting next to my wife and to my wife's cousin who was a hefty middle-aged woman who only wanted to talk about her numerous medical conditions and her home-based business of selling beauty products to all her friends and family.

After she made it though her gallstones, hot flashes, and ingrown toe nail, she started in on me to buy some of her men's skin care products. She looked at my face appraisingly and began to gush on and on about how I had the softest skin on my face and hands. She told me that she had never seen such wonderful skin on a man before and wanted to know what was my secret for my soft skin. I looked her straight in the eye and told her it was because I pissed in my bath water every day.

After a moment of stunned silence, my wife lit into me, and I decided that it was time for me to leave the house and wait in the car for her. Her whole family was lined up with her at the window watching me weave across the yard to the car. Unfortunately when I tried to jump the ditch by the road, I underestimated the power of the juniper berry, and I fell into the muddy ditch. Crawling out of the mud, I got into the back seat of the car and fell asleep.

When I woke up in the car the next morning, the car was parked in front of our house. I got out and tried to open our front door, but the chain was on the door and I couldn't get in. I rang the doorbell, and my wife came to the door and told me that she was through with me and my sorry, drunken behavior, that she was throwing me out of the house, and that I had to find somewhere else to live. Then, she shut the door and would not let me in our house.

That was two days ago, and I have been staying with a high school friend of mine and sleeping on his sofa with his big slobbery dog. I don't know if I want to stay married to my wife, but I don't want to move out of my house right now because I don't have anywhere to go and I can't afford to rent and furnish my own place.

To top it off, my wife changed the locks yesterday and won't let me back in and won't let me get any of my stuff.

Can my wife just throw me out of the house like that? How can I get back into my house without having World War III on my hands?


ANSWER: Even though you got drunk, were rude to her cousin, and embarrassed her in front of her entire family at the Christmas dinner, your wife has no legal right to keep you from staying at your house. The legal term for what she has done to you is called "malicious turning out of doors".

This house is the residence for both of you, and you are entitled to live at your house unless your wife gets a court order requiring you to leave.

So, you can get back into the house by hiring a locksmith and getting him to open the door for you. Then, you should have the locksmith change the locks so that you have a key to the new lock. Try to have the locksmith come when your wife is away from home at work, but if your wife is at home and starts raising Hail Columbia with you about being back, do not talk to her, just call the police and explain the situation.

You probably need to sleep in a different bedroom than your wife, and you definitely need to immediately get a good family law attorney because your marriage is apparently approaching the finish line.

Additionally, do not argue with your wife, yell at her, or threaten her because she will undoubtedly try to get you removed from your house with a domestic violence restraining order if you do any of these things.

Instead, abject apologies, roses, and Godiva chocolates for your wife and her cousin might be your best approach.  You also might try buying a hefty mea culpa order of men's skin care products from your wife's cousin, and for heaven's sake, keep any other "beauty" secrets that you might have to yourself!

# CHOOSE RIGHT